Before Buxton

The Muchakinock Years

Lee Ann Simmers Dickey

PBL Limited
Ottumwa, Iowa

Before Buxton: The Muchakinock Years
Copyright 2014 by Lee Ann Simmers Dickey
Cover and design copyright 2014 by Michael W. Lemberger

This edition published 2014

10 9 8 7 6 5 4 3 2 1

ISBN: 1892689545
ISBN 13: 9781892689542

Printed in the United States of America

Illustrations used with permission. Deb Anderson pages 26, 28; Traci Davis pages 51, 53; Lee Ann Simmers Dickey pages 6, 9, 22, 29, 32, 49, 55; Janice Dixon page 24; Kim Irvin-Carr pages 19, 20; Mahaska Historical Society page10; Robert Thompson pages 4, 43, 74; Joann Vestal pages 12, 16.

All rights reserved. Except for brief passages quoted in any review, the reproduction or utilization of this work in whole or in part, in any form or by any electronic, mechanical, or other means, now known or hereinafter invented, including xerography, photocopying and recording, or in any information storage and retrieval system, is forbidden without the express permission of the publisher. For permission contact:
    Rights Editor
    PBL Limited
    P.O. Box 935
    Ottumwa IA 52501-0935
    pbl@pbllimited.com

www.pbllimited.com for more information about this and other publications.

Before Buxton:

The Muchakinock Years
1874-1900

Before Buxton: The Muchakinock Years

Chicago and Northwestern (C N W) Railroad depot at Muchakinock, date not known.
(Courtesy of Robert Thompson)

LeeAnn Simmers Dickey

Author's Note

This book is dedicated to all the families who had ancestors who worked in the coal mines. It was a hard life full of accidents, illness, and very little pay. We would not be where we are today without the sacrifices they made for their families to have a better life.

I would like to thank Robert Thompson for all the help he has given me with my books. Also thanks to all the Buxton descendants, who have become very good friends to my family. As always thanks go to my family for all their continued support and encouragement. I wish to thank Kim Carr, Traci Davis, Janice Dixon, Deb Anderson, Joann Vestal and Robert Thompson for sharing photographs.

As many of you know, I am a genealogist and it is all about facts and proof of information. Make sure if you are looking for certain names in the records I have provided that you check all potential spellings. Listings are recorded here exactly as they were written back then, so you will find a lot of misspellings and spelling variations.

There is not a lot of information to be found on Muchakinock, and not many photographs have survived. Most of the information came from hours of reading newspapers from Eddyville and Oskaloosa. Another good source is the Iowa State Bystander newspaper.

I hope I have given you an idea of what the town of Muchakinock was like, along with the people in it. So many of these little towns are gone and forgotten, but they made a big impact in what has become the state we know today. Take pride in your ancestors and the hard work they put forth so you could have an easier life today. If it was not for them, you would not be here. Best wishes to all of you in your hunt for family information to pass down to the next generations!

— Lee Ann Simmers Dickey

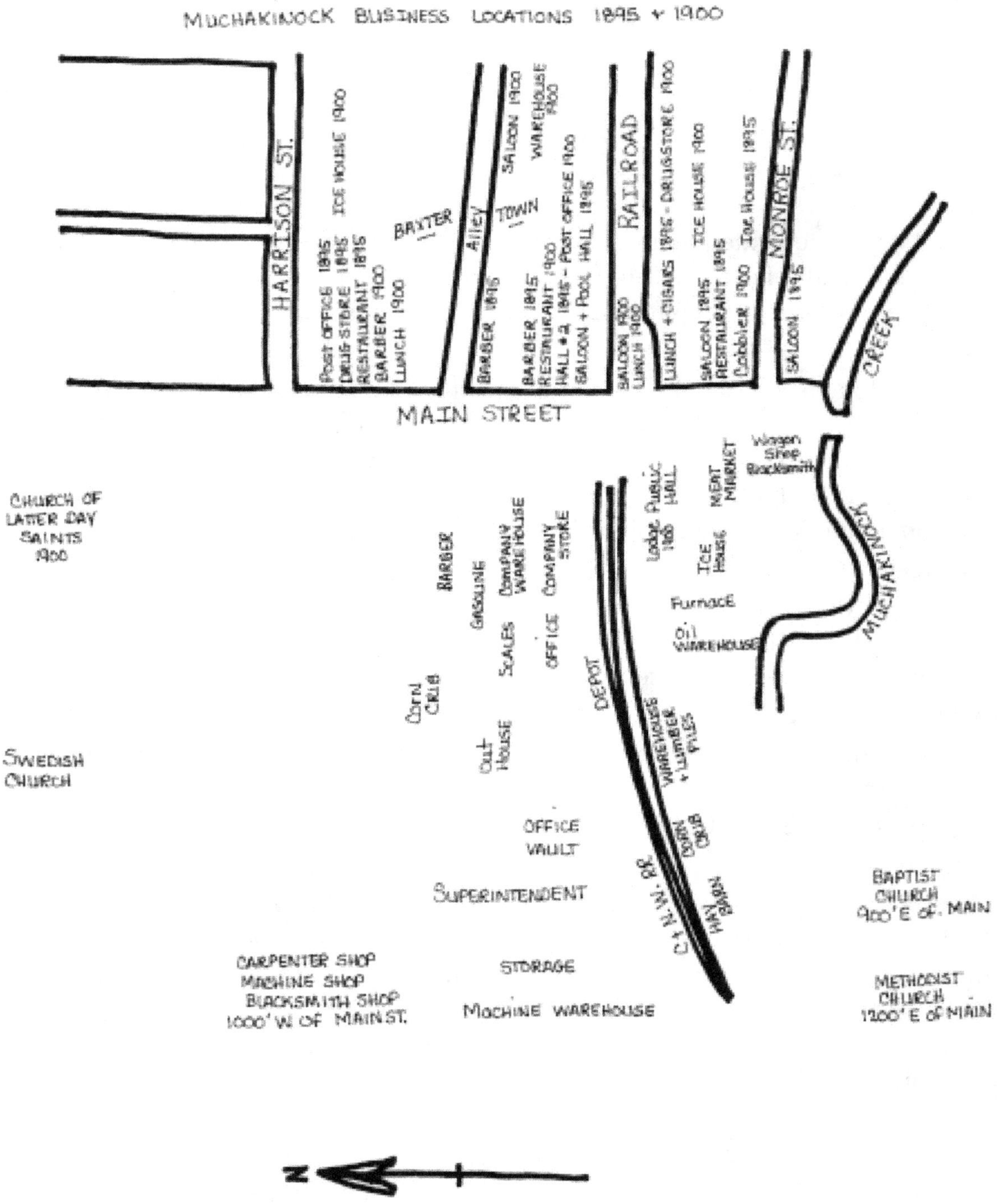

Before Buxton: The Muchakinock Years

Author's map showing business locations in Muchakinock. (Lee Ann Simmers Dickey)

LeeAnn Simmers Dickey

Table of Contents

Why Muchakinock? ~~ 8

Consolidation Coal Company ~~ 10

The Town of Muchakinock ~~ 15

The Town of Baxter ~~ 25

Well known Visitors and Residents ~~ 26

The Move to Buxton ~~ 30

Consolidation Coal Miners 1876 ~~ 31

Consolidation Coal Company Payroll Records 1880 ~~ 33

Recruiting Strikebreakers ~~ 50

Miners Killed in Muchakinock Mine Accidents ~~ 54

African-American Marriages of Mahaska County, Iowa 1880 - 1922 ~~ 56

Muchakinock Cemetery Records ~~ 75

Sources ~~ 88

About the Author ~~ 89

Before Buxton: The Muchakinock Years

Why Muchakinock?

Muchakinock, a small and unincorporated town located in Mahaska, County, Iowa from 1874 to about 1900, was one of many similar towns which existed in Iowa during the latter half of the nineteenth century, when coal was king and mining was one of the state's largest industries. What made Muchakinock unusual, especially for the time, was the high percentage of African-American residents there — miners and their families who were brought to Muchakinock by Consolidation Coal Company to work the coal seams.

The town of Muchakinock was first and foremost a company town. Established by Consolidation to house its headquarters and workers, Muchakinock lasted as long as the company flourished. When the nearby coal mines played out and Consolidation moved on, so did most of the residents – and even the structures – of Muchakinock. A few stayed behind, as did the cemetery ... and the records, buried in archives and crumbling newsprint.

Many of Muchakinock's residents moved to Buxton, Iowa, in Monroe County, where many of them once again mined coal, while others turned to other occupations. Though Buxton was both larger and better-known, it too became a ghost town when once more the mines were exhausted. Some families continued to follow the coal seams across Monroe County; others sought out other opportunities in cities like Des Moines, Cedar Rapids, Waterloo, and further afield.

But the memories of these coal-mining towns, and the unusual combination of black and white living and working side by side, live on.

Genealogist Lee Ann Simmers Dickey has long made a specialty of searching out the dusty and often tangled records of the black families of southeastern Iowa. In her previous books she assembled the birth, death, marriage, and census records of Buxton. Now she digs further into the past, bringing to light the lives of Muchakinock – nearly a century and a half after the town was founded.

-- *The Editors*

Muchakinock company store, date not known. (Lee Ann Simmers Dickey)

Before Buxton: The Muchakinock Years

Consolidation Coal Company

Wilbur A. McNeill was born in 1843 in Springfield, Illinois and gained his early education from the Sandstone Seminary. After finishing his schooling he went on to fight in the Civil War with the Fourth Illinois Calvary, and he was wounded in the hand at a skirmish in Memphis, Tennessee.

He became an entrepreneur in business, working at first for the coal mines in Monroe County before making his way into Mahaska County, Iowa in 1873. As he looked over the land, he established that there was a good source of coal under the rich farmland.

W. A. McNeill, along with his brother H. W. Neill, started the Iowa Central Coal Company with a capital investment of $100,000. Along with the McNeill brothers, J. K. Graves of Dubuque was also an owner.

The partners bought 800 acres of land in Mahaska County and opened mine No. 1. By 1876 they were shipping 55 to 65 railcar loads of coal per day. Coal was used for heating homes, for powering manufacturing plants, and by the railroads to fuel their steam locomotives.

Iowa Central Coal's payroll ranged from $13,000 to $16,000 per month. They annually shipped about 250,000 tons of coal.

View of Muchakinock and the coal mines, 1896. (Mahaska Historical Society archives)

LeeAnn Simmers Dickey

On January 6, 1876, the Iowa Central Coal Company, the Black Diamonds of Coalfield (Monroe County, Iowa), and The Eureka Mine (Beacon, Mahaska County, Iowa) were all merged into a new firm called Consolidation Coal Company.

The officers of the new company were: C. C. Gilman of Eldora, President; H. W. McNeill of Oskaloosa, General Superintendent; W. A. McNeill of Oskaloosa, Assistant Superintendent; J. W. Huggins of Ottumwa, Treasurer; John W. Gilman of Marshalltown, Secretary. C. P. Dandy went to work for Consolidation on April 9, 1881 as cashier and accountant.

The board of directors was made up of J. K. Graves of Dubuque; E. Clark of Iowa City; R. E. Finkbine of Des Moines; Hobart W. McNeill of Muchakinock; Tom Height of Coalfield and E. J. Evans of Beacon.

Not long after the merger, Ezekiel Clark became president of Consolidation Coal, and he soon noticed waste of product around the mines. He offered the slack (made up of very fine pieces of coal and coal dust) free to anyone who would erect the machinery to turn the waste material, often called nut coal, into coke, a high-carbon fuel with few impurities.

Coke, a solid product left behind when the volatile matters were expelled by distillation of bituminous coal, was said to be more economical and healthier than burning coal. Because the volatile portion of the coal was burned off in processing, coke did not smoke or flame, and therefore it left no residue on walls or hands.

H. A. McNeill accepted the offer, and the Muchakinock Coke Company was established in July 1877. Articles of incorporation were filed and recorded on August 22, 1877 in Mahaska County, Iowa. He erected the works at the cost of $10,000.

Directors of the company were Hobart W. McNeill, president; his brother Wilbur A. McNeill, secretary and treasurer; and John W. Gilman of Mason City, Iowa. The coke works was erected near Mine 1 adjoining the railroad switch, with a bank of twelve ovens.

The bank of ovens occupied a frontage of 80 feet, with a depth of 20 feet, and were about 9 feet high. The ovens consisted of around 4,000 fire bricks resting upon a solid stone foundation, which was laid with fire clay. The ovens were arched over the top to vent, and together they held about five ton of coal.

Waste coal was raised to the top of the ovens with an elevator and washed before going into the oven chambers. After the firing and cooling, the coke was stored in a warehouse measuring 30 x 100 feet, containing bins similar to wheat bins. After processing, the coke was a steely gray color. The ovens turned out about fifteen tons

Before Buxton: The Muchakinock Years

H. W. McNEILL, General Supt.   GEN'L SUPERINTENDENT'S OFFICE   W. A. McNEILL, Assistant Supt.

CONSOLIDATION COAL COMPANY,

MAHASKA CO.   Muchackinock, Iowa, March 1st 1876

Joseph Chilton Esqr;

    As I told you, the reduction in our force this spring makes it necessary for me to do without a foreman at No 1 exclusively, and this, of course terminates your connection with us at least for the present.

    You have been in our employ for about three years, in charge of No 1 the largest mine, I think, in Iowa.

    The most excellent condition in which you leave your work is your best testimonial of faithfulness & competency.

    Should you desire to engage in any other service before we can again offer you an engagement I will most cheerfully furnish you with any special endorsement that the most critical manager of mining property may demand. Believe me to be

Very Truly Yours
H. W. McNeill
Supt.

Letter sent by H. W. McNeill, superintendent of Consolidation Coal Company, to Joseph Chilton. Text is on page 13. A photograph of Joseph Chilton is on page 16. (Courtesy of Joann Vestal)

of coke daily, and the product sold at six to seven dollars per ton.

The Eddyville *Tribune* said that in May of 1878 the company began making tile from 1½ to 8 inches in diameter, because it could be baked in the same ovens using local clay.

By 1878 Consolidation Coal Co. had approximately 400 employees. The company owned around 3,000 acres of land in total. Some of the land was located in Hardin County, Iowa, as well as tracts in Mahaska County, Iowa.

In 1880 the company was sold to Chicago and Northwestern Railroad and began to produce coal exclusively for the railroad's use in powering steam locomotives. H. W. McNeill resigned his position with the company, and J. E. Buxton, Esq. of Boone, Iowa, took his place. The McNeill brothers sold the Consolidation Coal Company for $500,000 cash. W. A. McNeill went on to found the Oskaloosa Livery and Transfer Company.

Mines 1, 2, 3 and 5 were all in operation by 1884. By December of 1885, Mine No. 1 was worked out and no longer producing.

J. W. Nash filled the position as weigh master at Mine No. 2, along with John Roberts being foreman. In 1885, John Roberts moved to Mine No. 5 as foreman and

---

Muchakinock, Iowa, March 1st, 1876

Joseph Chilton, Esq:

As I told you, the reduction in our force this spring makes it necessary for me to do without a foreman at No 1 exclusively, and this, of course terminates your connection with us at least for the present.

You have been in our employ for about three years in charge of No 1, the largest mine, I think, in Iowa.

The most excellent condition in which you leave your work is your best testimonial of faithfulness and competency.

Should you desire to engage in any other service before we can again offer you an engagement I will most cheerfully furnish you with any special endorsement that the most critical manager of mining property may demand.

Believe me to be

Very Truly your friend,

H. W. McNeill

Supt.

Before Buxton: The Muchakinock Years

Mike Wright took over the position as foreman in Mine No. 2. Jesse Jones held the position as blacksmith for Mine No. 2. Two new boilers went in at Mine No. 5 in 1886 and the weigh master for that shaft was William Smith.

By 1886, the superintendent of the mines put a stop to elementary-aged school children working in the mines. Boys as young as 10 would work alongside their fathers in the coal mining industry. His reasoning for doing this task was to get them in school.

Mine No. 6, about three miles north of town, was opened around 1884. The extension of the railroad to Mine No. 6 started in April of 1888, when the shaft was at a depth of 100 feet and was producing coal in record time. By 1893 there were 489 men and boys were working in Mines No. 6 and 7.

Oliver H. Vance was the weigh master at Mine No. 7. It was finished by January of 1900, but work in No. 7 ended almost as soon as it began. Water started running in fast, and it became too dangerous to work. The men were transferred to Mine No. 8, located about three miles northwest of Muchakinock, and Mine No. 9. There was not enough coal left in Mine No. 7 to worry about the water coming in.

John Roberts had taken over the position of superintendent, to replace J. W. McMillian. John Roberts resigned April 1, 1904, after 24 years of service with the company.

Jacob Olson was the master mechanic for Consolidation Coal Company, and the big fan that was used to furnish fresh air into the shaft was known as the "Olson Cage."

By 1904, the company had taken all the coal they could take out of the mines in Muchakinock. The mines and the town of Muchakinock closed down for good in May of 1904. The last remaining employees were sent to Buxton or Hocking, in Monroe County, Iowa.

LeeAnn Simmers Dickey

The Town of Muchakinock

The land which became the town of Muchakinock started out as a summer village of the Sac and Fox Indians. It was named for the creek that flowed through the valley, with the area known as the Muchakinock Creek Valley. The Indians believed that the cyclones would not cross the creek.

Muchakinock was established August 10, 1874. Initially known as Coal Valley, the town was laid out in the South West corner of the West half of Section 7, in West Des Moines Township in Mahaska County, Iowa -- about 5 miles south of Oskaloosa.

The original spelling was Muchackinock with an extra C, but the name was changed on December 4, 1886. The population around 1876 in this little town was 800 to 1,000 residents. It soon became the state's largest unincorporated coal mining community and also the largest settlement for African Americans. The town was not surveyed and platted until 1877.

The lots were irregular in width but the length ran any place between 120 to 200 feet. The surveyor certified the town was marked properly on July 9, 1877.

On July 12, 1877, the owners of the land gave their consent to use this area as a village to house the miners, as well as giving Consolidation Coal Company the right to mine out the coal which lay under the farmland. H. W. McNeill signed for Consolidation Coal Company. The land owners signing were James and Caroline Bones; Francis and Janet Chambers; James and Mary Chambers; John and Augusta Olson; John and Thea Dahn; Jacob and Ellen Olson; John and Mary E. Duggan; and M. G. Thomas.

The plat of the town was recorded in December of 1877.

Rather than using official street names, areas of the town were referred to as New Town, Swede Patch, Brown Row, Givin Avenue, Brides Row, Red Row or Mine No. 3, 5, 6, 7, 8, and 9. Both the Chicago & North Western and the Keokuk & Des Moines railroad tracks ran within a few hundred yards of the town.

The town was unincorporated and governed by three Township trustees, two justices of the peace and two constables. The main part of town was quite small with a lot of house and outlying areas that surrounded it.

The white sector of the settlement was west of the main roadway between Oskaloosa and Eddyville. The half-mile strip east of the main road was given over to the African-American population.

Before Buxton: The Muchakinock Years

A large population of Swedish miners lived in a settlement on top of the hill north of Slope No. 2, with a line of houses on both sides of the road leading from the main road west to Givin, Iowa – an area which became known as Swede Row.

H. W. Mc Neill built a framed, two-story house (35 feet square), with a 35 feet high tower on a little plateau near his office. Located at the back of the house on the hillside was a spring of water, which was piped through the house. He also built a fountain in front of the house which threw water twenty feet high. A rock basement was built under the whole building.

Armstrong's meat market was just south of the town hall, and O. H. Vance also operated a meat market. John Burt had a meat shop in 1881.

The doctors in town were Dr. Joshua S. Henderson and Dr. J. E. Morgan. By 1884, Dr. Henderson also operated a drugstore from his office on the main street. The custodian of his office was "Doc" Southall, and Benny Green was his driver. The thoroughbred horses raised by Hobe Armstrong were used by the doctor.

"Old Lady Ross" (no other name is recorded) was the midwife in town.

B. F. Cooper was the pharmacist. At this time he was noted as one of the only two African-American pharmacists in the state of Iowa.

The only attorney in town was George H. Woodson, who lived in a beautiful home known as "Bachelors' Park Home". Professor S. Joe Brown was his personal secretary.

W. C. (William Channing) Perdue and company were the main merchants in town from 1873 to about 1878. The average sales in the Perdue store were $6,000 to $8,000 per month.

In 1878, the general store was run by Little, Kelly and Company. Sales from the general store were around $50,000 per year, with stock

Joseph Chilton, foreman of Mine No. 1, with daughter Martha Emily Chilton. (Courtesy of Joann Vestal)

invested to nearly $9,000. The store carried everything from lumber to food, clothing and more. Produce was often exchanged for goods.

Wm. F. Little was a liveryman, and he also was a bookkeeper from June 1878 to August 1881 for Little, Kelly and Company. Frank Kelly then sold his interest in the general store to S. T. Blade.

James Martin was a barber in 1884, with his shop located across from the company store. Mr. Martin was quoted as saying, "I am white in principle but my skin is a little dark. My blood is as white as the next one but I was born free."

The Union Hotel was advertised in the Oskaloosa Weekly Herald on July 8, 1880: "The manager, Taylor Jefferson, is an old hotel keeper of Virginia. Meals at all hours, boarding and lodging by day or by week and keeper of confectionary and cigars."

Rhodes livery stable and bus transportation ran a bus line between Muchakinock and Oskaloosa. It was established in August of 1886.

Just north of the town was the location of the Muchakinock Yards where the railroad roundhouse stood, along with the post office.

In 1888, a hotel was operated at the yards by Jones and Preastly.

The Muchakinock Post Office was established August 10, 1874 with Hobart W. McNeill as postmaster. Other postmasters were: John E. Buxton – appointed May 31, 1881; Joshua S. Henderson -- May 11, 1886; Noah Greenway -- December 20, 1886; Nathan B. McDowell -- April 27, 1889; Florence P. Cook -- January 9, 1890; Benjamin F. Phillips -- December 17, 1890; Henry Alde -- August 8, 1894; Anderson Perkins -- July 11, 1898. In 1887 the deputy postmaster was Mr. Snow of Eddyville. The post office was discontinued June 15, 1904.

The Muchakinock State was a new newspaper in 1897, with Mr. J. E. White as manager.

W.D. Crawford opened an ice cream parlor in May 1897.

Baxter and Armstrong Livery Stable was a business in town.

The Gladwin house was located about a quarter mile north of Swede Row. The Gladwins ran a hack line — the equivalent of today's taxis -- to Oskaloosa. Mr. Gladwin made several trips with horses and wagon a day, so that miners and their families would have a way to go to town for shopping and entertainment.

A two-story billiard hall was owned by Noah Greenway. This building adjoined the Baxter and Armstrong livery stable, and adjoining the billiard hall was the drugstore owned by Noah Greenway.

Before Buxton: The Muchakinock Years

Elerick Drugstore was located in the Star Co. building and opened in 1897. Joe Ellerick had formerly worked for Greenway Drug. Elerick Drugstore was sold in 1899 to J. F. Noel of Chicago.

W. P. Jones had a saloon and restaurant. Mrs. Sam Meese ran the restaurant out of the back of the saloon.

Mrs. Alice Massey ran the Muchakinock Bakery and Restaurant until April of 1900 when she sold out to Mrs. Anderson Perkins. Ice cream was also sold there.

By the end of the 1900s, some of the other businesses included Ad Rhodes shoe shop, located in a building owned by Jack Baxter; the Muchakinock Drug Co.; J.E. Williams' restaurant; the Muchakinock Opera House.

A dressmaking parlor was opened on Swede Row by Stella Armstrong.

John Baxter had the icehouse.

Mr. Moore was the police officer in Muchakinock.

Mr. Coleman and Mrs. Page Irwin, Churchman Tyler, and Baxter Quarles all had boarding houses.

William T. Cross was a blacksmith.

Fires

Fire swept through the town numerous times, and some of the buildings were destroyed more than once and rebuilt. A lot of these buildings were not covered by insurance, because the rate in Muchakinock was very high. Most of the businesses did not have fire walls to separate the structures and they were constructed of wood, which made them more of a risk for fire.

The biggest fires in town occurred in 1881, 1898, and 1900.

In September of 1881, Baxter and Armstrong livery stable (28 by 62 feet) was discovered to be on fire. Located next to it was a two-story billiard hall (44 x 24 feet) owned by Noah Greenway. The next building was the drug store owned by Noah Greenway, which had minimal damage. Insurance was carried on the livery. Rebuilding began immediately on the livery and billiard hall.

In January of 1898, the business district on the east side of Muchakinock was almost totally destroyed by fire. The fire started in Jack Baxter's saloon. It destroyed everything in the Odd Fellows' building and north to the Carey Barber Shop. The Greenway building was also destroyed. The Elerick Drug Store and W.P. Jones Saloon and restaurant, just south of Baxter's saloon, were also damaged. Rebuilding began in February.

LeeAnn Simmers Dickey

Lewis Arthur Burkett
(Courtesy of Kim Irvin-Carr)

In December of 1900, a fire started in the saloon owned by W. P. Jones. It destroyed the saloon and restaurant owned by Jones, a shoe shop owned by Addison Rhodes, a restaurant owned by J. E. Williams, the saloon and residence of Jack Baxter, along with the Muchakinock Drug Company. The Opera House was damaged, along with Hobe Armstrong's meat market.

Churches

Muchakinock offered two white churches (Methodist and Baptist), the Swede Church on Swede Row (Lutheran), and Sunday school open to all denominations. The resident pastor for the Methodist Church was Rev. L. H. Reynolds; pastor of the Union Baptist Church was Rev. W. J. Barnett. Rev. T. L. Griffith was in charge of the "Colored" Baptist church. There was also a Methodist Church for the African-Americans. The annual baptizing ceremony took place in the big pond near the town above Mine No. 2.

A church was also reportedly built by the Congregationalists.

Schools

Samuel J. Brown, a principal in the Muchakinock schools, was the first African-American to receive a bachelor's degree from the State University of Iowa.

Teachers at Muchakinock schools were: Miss Emma Sciple, Miss Clara Lacy, Miss Emma D. Metler, Miss Lizzie S. Barber (String Four School), Miss Salina E. Pugh (Excelsior School), Mr. Larkin, Mr. John Ruan, Miss Lessie Larkin (East Muchakinock School), Lizzie Phillips (Swede Row School), Mr. S. Joe Brown (East Des Moines Township School), Miss Sarah A. Pointer (East Des Moines Township School).

Before Buxton: The Muchakinock Years

John Carr
(Courtesy of Kim Irvin-Carr)

The principal at the African-American primary school was Mr. L. A. Wiles. The teacher, Miss Alice Anderson, was the only African-American teacher in the county.

All of the schools in the district were presented flags and flagpoles by Ben Buxton on Nov 12, 1898.

The Swede Row schoolhouse was adjacent to the main road at the east end of Swede Row. On December 10, 1898 the Swede Row School was closed due to an outbreak of diphtheria.

Clubs and Entertainment

The community built a park and named it Woodson Park, with the band playing every Thursday night as entertainment.

A number of musical organizations were organized at various times in Muchakinock.

In 1879, the members of the Muchakinock Cornet Band Black Diamonds were listed as Moses Northway, Leader; William Moyle, B Flat; Henry John, Solo Trombone; Thomas Grose, Solo Baritone; Samuel Cresswell, Second Baritone; John Lloyd, Solo Alto; Thomas Farley, Second Alto; John Moyle, B Bass; John Lyne, Tuba; Dan Harry, Bass Drum; Fred Kelly, Side Drum.

The Oskaloosa newspaper said, "The fancy uniforms were furnished by Morris L. Levi and were a beautiful dark steel gray, with gold cord trimming down the seams of the pants, a cutaway coat trimmed with gold cord, white linen standup collar, and a row of brass buttons that buttoned all the way up to the throat. The cap is a forage pattern, one shade lighter than the suit, surmounted by a white stub plume."

In 1898, the Muchakinock Cornet Band was said to be the oldest and best colored musical organization in Iowa.

It was first organized in the spring of 1880 in Staunton, Virginia through the efforts of Geo. Lewis and John Orpin. It consisted then of 15 pieces with the following officers: Frank Woodard, President; R. S. Brown, Secretary; Churchman Taylor, Treasurer;

and Geo. Lewis, Instructor. They advanced rapidly, considering more than half were unacquainted with music before joining.

Mr. Lewis was succeeded by Mr. Orpin as instructor. Later R. S. Brown was elected director, a position he held until he went to Chicago to attend the Medical College. Then J. R. McDowell was elected. Other directors were F. G. Grogging and Lewis Landon.

The Iowa Bystander newspaper in December of 1898 listed the members as: Lewis London, B flat cornet; H. C. Lee, 2nd B flat cornet; Chas. Brooks, E flat clarinet; Ben Tate, B flat clarinet; Joe Tate, B flat clarinet; John Rhodes, B flat clarinet; Leaford Willis, B flat cornet; Lewis Perkins, saxophone; Ed. Miles, solo alto; James Jones, alto; Peter Cary, alto; E. A. London, 1st slide trombone; Wm. Reasby, 2nd trombone; Thos. Turner, tenor; Wm. Thomas, E. D. Blakey, bass; J. H. McDobell, bass; Ben Green, snare drum; Fred Drew, bass drum; M. O. Henderson, drum major; Lucian Cary, property man. Officers were Peter Cary, President; E. A. London, Secretary; Lewis London, Treasurer.

In addition to the cornet band, other bands included the Juvenilian Brass Band, organized and instructed by John Orpin, and a brass band organized by white musicians, which consisted of 18 pieces with Joseph Poole as the leader.

Muchakinock Glee Club was under the leadership of Tom Reese, with 33 members.

Northwestern Choral Union practiced their singing two to three times a week for concerts.

The Odd Fellows' building was owned by a company consisting of John Green, B. F. Cooper, John Chatman, Dave Thomas, and C. R. Foster and was located on the second floor of B. F. Cooper's drugstore.

The I.O.O.F. chapter was known as Phallin Lodge No. 602 and No. 609.

G.W.O. of F. (Known as "Household of Ruth", No. 312). Members included: Mrs. L. D. Walker, Mrs. E. W. Lewis, Mrs. Martha C. Clark, Mrs. Amelia Cary, Rev. W. M. Wood, Miss Sallie A. Jones, F. H. Carter, J. H. Bates, J. H. Lewis, E. N. Tyrell. Known today as the Grand United Order of Odd Fellows. To assist the needy, sick, and distressed. It was for women and wives related to men in the Fraternal Order of the Odd Fellows.

The Progressive Golden League club was for the members to get better acquainted with the best authors. The officers were: Miss Carrie Thomas, President; W. H. London, Vice-President; Miss Cora Thomas, Secretary; Rev. T. L. Griffith, Corresponding Secretary; Mrs. Lenora Cannady, Treasurer; and Scott Walker, Critic. The members

Before Buxton: The Muchakinock Years

included Mrs. W. H. London, John Drew, Luther Brown and Mrs. Jennie Brooks.

In 1885, members and officers of Cedar Grove Lodge No. 4, A.F.A.M. (Ancient Free and Accepted Masons) included L. H. Reynolds, Worshipful Master; John L. Bedell, Senior Warden; Phillip C. Fairfax, Junior Warden; W. J. Jackson, Treasurer; John H. McDowell, Secretary; W. A. Searcy, Senior Deacon; Sam Wilson, Junior Deacon; Will Jones, Senior Steward; Charles Mease, Junior Steward; Jeff Thurman, Tyler; Al Jewett, Chaplain.

Mystic Shrine of Colored Masons was established in April of 1900 by Isaac L. Brown, of Marshalltown, who was the Grand Master of the state of Iowa, A.F. & A.M., with the installment of 42 members.

Zion Rebekah Lodge 361 surrendered their charter in April of 1899.

Virginia Queen Court officers included Mrs. Addie Johnson; Mrs. C. R. Brookings; W. D. Crawford; Mrs. Martin Jackson; Miss Jennie Brooks; Mrs. Julia Southall; Sampson Johnson; M. E. Panel; T. A. Coleman and Mrs. Mary Mease.

Public Halls in town included Baxter Hall, Harris Hall and Odd Fellows Hall. There was also a library.

Other organizations which existed in Muchakinock but about which little is known include the Muchakinock Guards, which were performing by 1883; the Black Diamond Baseball Club, Reynolds' Masonic Lodge U.D.A.F.A.M., and the Knights of Pythias.

The African-American families had Anniversary Balls and celebrations for their arrival in Muchakinock. Concerts, plays, speeches, fairs, and dances were big entertainment for the families, with the whole town turning out for some of the major events.

When in Muchakinock, Iowa, stop at MRS. ADDIE JOHNSON'S RESTAURANT for good meals or short orders; also Ice Cream. Prompt attention given to all orders.

The Muchakinock Fair was known to everyone as one of the biggest celebrations of the year, with crowds of 3,000 to 4,000 people. Hobart A.

Advertisement from the *Iowa State Bystander* newspaper (Lee Ann Simmers Dickey)

LeeAnn Simmers Dickey

Armstrong was president of the Association and John McDowell served as secretary.

The fair was held at the Muchakinock driving Park a half-mile west of Mr. Armstrong's residence. Admission for the fair was one quarter. The horse races were held on Hobe Armstrong's third-of-a mile track and were one of the major draws to the fair. At one side was the betting booths, with signs of $1.00, $5.00, $10.00, $25.00 and $50.00 above the windows.

On the left side were stands and concessions of novelties and food stands.

A big building called Floral Hall displayed exhibits of fruit, flowers, canned goods, needlework and handcrafted items. At night the tables were moved against the wall and the orchestra played, with the floor filling with dancers. Different brass and cornet bands played. There was an art hall, and trapshooting.

Lunch and fruit stands were scattered all over the grounds, with soda pop and other refreshments served.

In 1887 at the 4th of July celebration the Sunday school formed a procession led by the band at 10 a.m. and marched to the grove. At the grove was a barbeque of 800 pounds of meat which included veal, mutton, pork and vegetables. Contributions made for the barbeque came from J. E. Buxton, S. T. Slade and H. A. Armstrong.

The Muchakinock Fair would last anywhere from three days to a week, and was bigger than the Mahaska County Fair.

Before Buxton: The Muchakinock Years

Martha Swann Reasby Shepard.
(Courtesy of Janice Dixon)

The Town of Baxter

The town of Baxter was located inside the town limits of Muchakinock. Jack Baxter was the founder of the small town, which was referred to as the smallest incorporated town in the world, with a frontage of 558½ feet abutting on the highway and a depth of 75 feet, with lots extending eastward.

The incorporation of the town resulted when the coal company thought Baxter's Saloon was getting too much of the miners' money and tried to shut it down.

Iowa was one of the first states to adopt prohibition laws, going partly dry in 1855 and more completely in 1885. Within the first two years of Muchakinock's existence there were two saloons established, and within the next 10 years this grew to a total of eight saloons. With the prohibition laws and a little help from the women in town, all the saloons had closed their doors by July of 1884. Between 1885 and 1919, Iowa loosened restrictions on alcohol sales and use, but in 1919 the Volstead Act (National Prohibition Act) went into effect.

In January of 1894, the 25th General Assembly of Iowa adapted the Mulct Law. This legislation taxed the liquor traffic, and under certain conditions, protected saloons from the enforcements of the penalties of the prohibitory liquor law. The saloon keepers had to procure the written consent of the majority of the voters in the city for the establishment to operate, as well as paying an annual tax for the saloon. Under the provisions of the Mulct Law, Baxter could form his own town and keep his saloon operating.

The town of Baxter held its first election of officers with a full quota. Jack Baxter served as mayor and was the only white official on the slate. Also elected were a clerk, treasurer, assessor, and six councilmen. Their office was located in a two-story men's rooming house, referred to by the locals as "The Ark". The town of Baxter had less than a dozen residents and it was sustained by the taxes of three Mulct Law saloons. The three saloons were each paying $600 in taxes a year.

Several suits were brought to court to vacate the town of Baxter and to dissolve the incorporation, claiming that under the code of a town there must be at least 25 voters before it could be incorporated. In January of 1897, a new trial for the dissolution was ordered by Judge Ryan, and sometime after that trial the town of Baxter ceased to exist.

Before Buxton: The Muchakinock Years

Famous Residents and Visitors

Booker T. Washington, the famous African-American educator and author, made several trips to Muchakinock to lecture and inspire the people. The mines and businesses were closed for the day. A scholarship was presented to Miss Blanche White, an accomplished young African-American girl, by the Mahaska County Iowa Farmers Institute. The seats were full at the Central Methodist Church with 1,200 people turning out to hear Mr. Washington speak.

Edward Carter graduated from the Oskaloosa High School in 1899 and was the first Muchakinock resident to attend the University of Iowa. He later went to medical school and became a physician in Buxton.

Samuel J. Brown was one of the principals of the Muchakinock schools. He was also the first African-American to receive a bachelor's degree from the State University of Iowa.

One of the best-known residents of Muchakinock and later of Buxton was **Hobart A. (Hobe) Armstrong,** who was a prosperous merchant in Muchakinock and Buxton.

In November of 1876, he built a house in Muchakinock that was 18 feet x 24 feet. He erected a rigging so that he could pump water by wind to his large herd of stock. He owned a large meat market in Muchakinock and in Buxton after moving there in 1901.

Hobart A. (Hobe) Armstrong, said to be the richest black man in Iowa. (Courtesy of Deb Anderson)

After moving to Buxton he turned a building into one of the finest slaughterhouses in the state. He had a head for business and prospered over the years, not only financially but as a citizen and a leader in the community.

Mr. Armstrong was one of the largest land owners in southern Iowa, holding more than 1600 acres of land in southern Mahaska County and northern Monroe County. He was very enthusiastic about agricultural fairs and horse racing. Not only did he establish and operate the Muchakinock Fair but he backed Oskaloosa Exposition with both financial and personal assistance. Hobart Armstrong and William Griffin jointly owned and maintained the fairgrounds of Albia. He bred racehorses that could be found on almost every Iowa track and his stables included some of the fastest pacing and trotting horses that Iowa ever produced.

He was recorded as being mulatto, and claimed he was only 1/8 black. At the time it was claimed he was the richest black man in Iowa.

Oskaloosa *Daily Herald,* Thursday, November 5, 1932, Page 5 Column 2

Hobart A. Armstrong

Hobart A. Armstrong was born in Knoxville, Tennessee on April 9, 1851, and died at his home in Buxton Tuesday, October 18, 1932, aged 81 years 5 months and 9 days. His parents died when he was still an infant and as a small boy he came to Iowa with his foster parents, Dr. and Mrs. Ann Purdue, who preceded him in death. He was married to Ida A. Gladwin, May 23, 1873 in Ottumwa, Iowa. And to this union were born twelve children, one child died in infancy. Mr. and Mrs. Armstrong made their home near old Muchakinock, a once flourishing coal camp, where Mr. Armstrong operated a successful meat market. In 1901 he moved his family to Buxton where he was engaged in a similar enterprise and where he spent the remainder of his life. His wife, Ida, preceded him in death on November 7, 1898, and one daughter, Miss Lottie Armstrong died in April 1921. Mr. Armstrong is survived by 10 children: Charles W., Estella E., Ida A., Anna M., Hobart Jr., Ralph H., Arthur C., Nettie, Ethel A., and J. Emory Armstrong; 15 grandchildren and 3 great grandchildren. Funeral services were conducted from the Armstrong Home at 1:00 Friday afternoon, October 21, with Rev. O. M. Morgan officiating. Burial was made by the side of his wife in the Eddyville Cemetery.

Before Buxton: The Muchakinock Years

Ida Gladwin Armstrong, wife of Hobe Armstrong. (Courtesy of Deb Anderson)

Mr. Armstrong's parents, according to the 1925 census, were A. W. Armstrong, born in Ireland, and Mary McMillan, born in Tennessee. They passed away when he was very young and he was raised by Dr. Charles A. Perdue and his wife Ann Viola Munks. The family migrated to Iowa in 1872 and remained until 1878. The Perdues then went on to Kansas where they passed away. They only had one son, William Channing Perdue, who managed the company store in Muchakinock. William married Sarah "Sadie" Acheson of Monroe County and eventually left Iowa.

Hobart and his family members are buried in the Highland Cemetery, Eddyville, Iowa, in family lots 36 and 37 in the new section block 1.

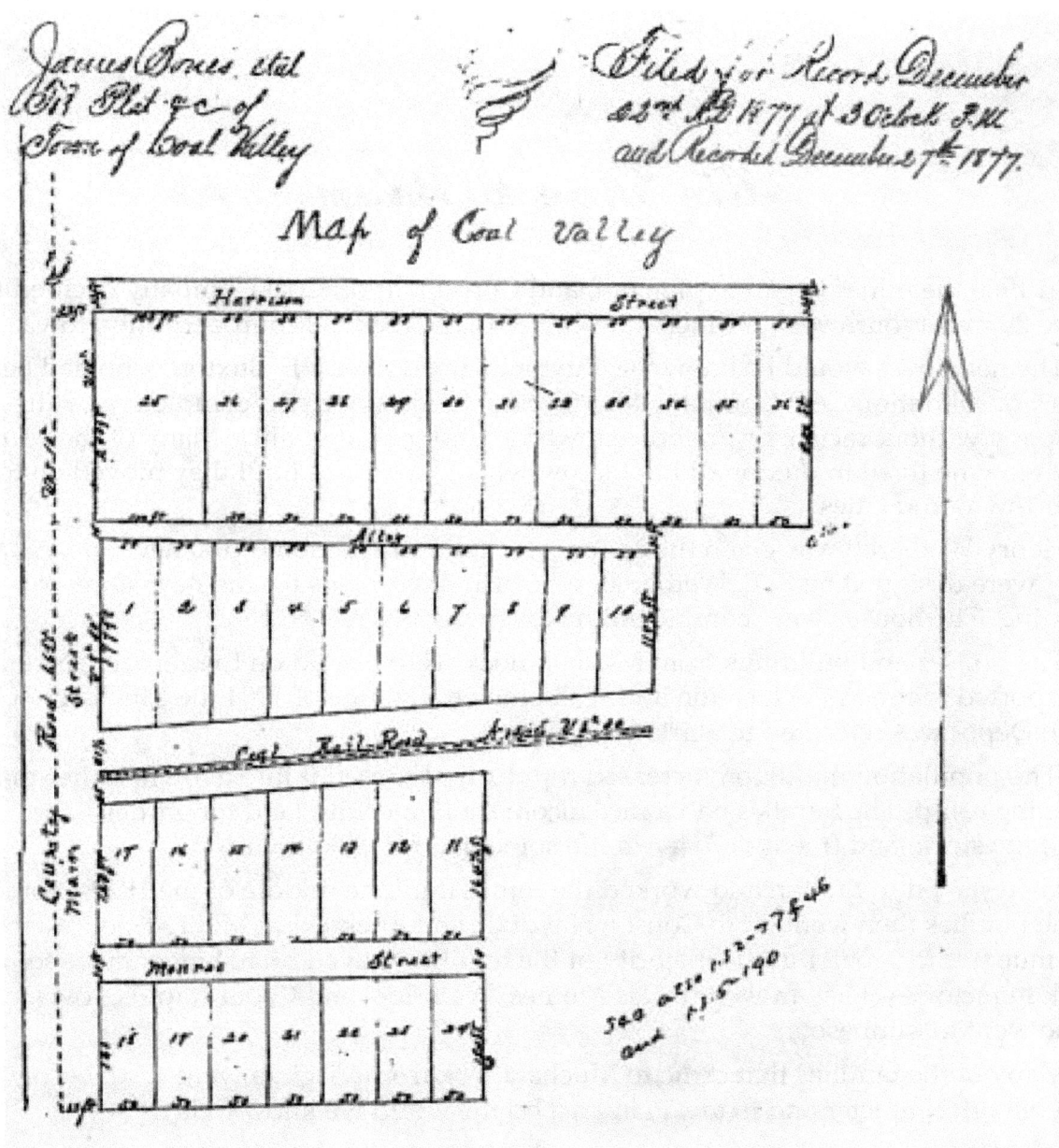

Original plat map of Coal Valley (later renamed Muchakinock), recorded at the Mahaska County Courthouse on December 27, 1877. Though street names seem not to have been used in Muchakinock, the plat shows Harrison Street and Monroe Street, as well as the railroad tracks and an alley. (Lee Ann Simmers Dickey)

Before Buxton: The Muchakinock Years

The Move to Buxton

In 1900 the mines began to play out, and Consolidation Coal Company decided to move 20 miles southwest of Muchakinock, to Bluff Creek in Monroe County, Iowa.

The new town would be known as Buxton, named after J. E. Buxton, who had been with Consolidation Coal Company for 20 years. It was governed completely by the company without racism or prejudice towards color or nationality. Many of the young children who lived in Buxton did not know what racism was until they moved on to other towns and cities.

Henry Wetherell was given the contract for the construction of 100 new houses. They were designed by F. E. Wetherell, who also drew plans for the new store building. The houses were completed in November of 1900.

The houses and buildings from Muchakinock were loaded on to railroad cars and transported to their new location and reassembled. By June of 1904 the Muchakinock Train Depot was relocated to Stark.

The population in Buxton increased rapidly and turned it into a town, rather than a mining camp. The families had a nice income, a home with land for gardens and small livestock, and freedom to live a life some had never known.

They stayed in Buxton and worked the mines until the middle of the 1920s. Some of the families then went on to Consol, Haydock and Bucknell in Monroe County to continue mining coal. But the majority of the families moved on to bigger cities to work in factories. They moved to Des Moines, Waterloo, and Cedar Rapids, Iowa. Some went to Minnesota.

Many of the families that came to Muchakinock from Virginia went on to become men of high character and made an impact on the world we know today.

LeeAnn Simmers Dickey

Consolidation Coal Miners 1876

Miners in 1876 that worked in Mine No. 1, Mine No. 2 and Mine No. 3 were:

Mine No. 1 -- Tobias Anderson, Dick Ashman, Sam Ashman, William Ballinger, Daniel Baxter, David Baxter, John Baxter, Mike Boroney, Ben Bosley, William Britton, George Brown, George Buchanan, James Bulger, John Bulger, Thomas Bulger, Joe Burdess, A. Butler, William Butler, B.F. Carter, Thomas Cary, Jake Creigler, Jim Crow, Michael Cummings, Frank Daily, E.J. Davis, I.K. Davis, Jerry Davis, John T. Davis, Robert Davis, Sam Davis, John Dugan, J. Dunn, D.B. Edwards, D.W. Edwards, George Ellis, D.J. Evans, James Foley, James Fox, Mike Fox, William Gaffney, John Griffin, Mike Huff, Evan Hughes, J.E. Hughes, Pat Hurley, J.D. Jenkins, William Jenkins, John Johnson, E. Jones, J.K. Jones, J.W. Jones, Jack Jones, Sol Jones, W.J. Jones, Thomas Kearney, George Kennedy, Dan Lafever, D.R. Lewis, Morris Lloyd, Charles McCarty, Pat McGill, D. McGrath, Neil McLaughlin, Pat McMann, John McNulty, J. Morgan, James Morgan, Thomas Morgan, D. Morris, Dick Morris, Joseph Morris, Thomas Morris, A.C. Nelson, John O'Harrow, John Orr, Alex Penman, T.D. Reese, J.D. Richards, William Ring, Frank Roach, William Roach, Lewis Roberts, John Rodgers, J. Roney, T. Rosser, John Shepherd, H. Stanton, John Stanton, Pat Stanton, A.A. Tedroe, Asa Thomas, D.H. Thomas, J.J. Thomas, Richard Thomas, Joseph Thrapp, William Titus, Andrew Vass, William Walker, Joseph Waller, Dan Whitsell, Jap Whitsell, M. Whitsell, James Wignall, Dave Williams, E.B. Williams, J.G. Williams, Jap Williams, John Williams, Richard Williams, Thomas Williams, W.E. Williams, P.C. Wilson, Thomas Wright, John Young.

Mine No. 2 -- Wash. Acton, John Bailey, Sam Bailey, William Bailey, Marion Belzer, Milton Belzer, Stephen Belzer, Frank Brasfield, John Burt, Ed Clark, Tom Delaney, Thomas Ellis, Ed Gladwin, Noah Greenway, Ike Jenkins, D.W. Jones, Dan Lafever, William McCamey, H. McGlasson, Morris Morris, John Orr, William Phillips, H. Pugh, Ed Roberts, J.C. Smith, Matt Sparks, W.C. Suggett, Evan Thomas, George Thrapp, H. Thrapp, Joseph Thrapp, H. Tullis, E. Weise, Sam Weise, H. Whitsell, Evan Williams.

Mine No. 3 -- Hobart Armstrong, George Ashman, Thomas Ashman, William Ashman, John Bash, L. Bernard, Dennis Burns, John Burt, Frank Carte, Martin Carter,

Before Buxton: The Muchakinock Years

Dick Chambers, F. Chambers, H. Chambers, James Chambers, James Conners, William Crews, E.J. Crow, John Dahn, John Dewey, C. Dixon, John Dolton, John Dowe, John Ellison, Dick Evans, E. Evans, Frank Fletcher, Alf Greenway, William Greenway, H. Griffith, Robert Hughes, Charles Johnson, Charles McCarty, Pat McGovern, David Morgan, John Oleson, William Phillips, Charles Piper, Robert Piper, Dave Quirk, L. Rice, John E. Richards, D.M. Roy. Tom Scott, George Simms, J.T. Smith, Pete Smith, James Stanton, W. Suggett, Con Sullivan, Morgan Thomas, Sil Totman, Agnew Vance, T. Victor, John Watkins, John Weise, J.A. White, I.W. Whitesell, James Wilkerson Jr., Ben Williams, Jink Williams, L. Zering, W. Zering.

View of Muchakinock showing a mine in the foreground, date not known. (Lee Ann Simmers Dickey)

LeeAnn Simmers Dickey

Payroll records for Consolidation Coal Company March 1880

Terry, John		$55.26
Bloomfield, Chas.		$61.23
Chambers, Francis		$62.23
Penman, Alex.		$114.63
Blackstone, J. W and Co.		$49.20
Blazier, David		$47.37
Lewis, John J.		$47.37
Calsan, Alex.		$75.54
Quist, Andrew		$75.54
Burdess, William		$69.84
Titus, William D.		$118.38
Williams, J. G. & Son	Trapping	$93.97
McLaughlin, N.	Driving	$76.21
McMahn, Pat	Trapping	$78.06
Weese, E. and Co.		$99.06
Roberts, Lewis		$84.69
Wilson, P. C. and Co.		$139.08
Dahn, John		$82.71
Oleson, John		$82.71
Bulger, John		$67.26
Johnson, Wm.		$73.92
Swanson, Nelson	Moving Slate	$74.92
Baxter, Jack		$19.56
Humphry, Muck		$8.49
Nicholson, Dorn	Watching	$59.16
Moore, Jake		$55.14
Reesor, John		$29.97
Jones, Wm. J.		$62.16
Roberts, Edwin		$76.02
Moyle, John		$29.07
Carney, Tom	Setting Posts	$79.94
Dewey, John	Setting Posts	$79.94

Before Buxton: The Muchakinock Years

Chilton, Abram		$105.84
Cherrington, Wm.	Driving and Setting Posts	$115.10
Mobley, Rich and Co.		$81.78
Robinson, D. A.		$57.96
Hendricks, Alf		$58.47
Rogers, Jack and Co.	Trapping	$100.02
Williams, Ed O.		$81.66
Northway, Mose		$39.81
Morris, Morris		$70.14
Anderson, Albert		$6.18
Anderson, Nelson		$6.18
Mobbley, Lon		$43.83
Mobbley, James		$45.63
Knight, David		$39.72
Lee, Olloff		$6.42
Anderson, Elias		$6.42
Anderson, Chas. & Son		$3.63
Edwards, David		$84.99
Grose, Thomas		$79.62
Cadle, John		$.72
Wright, Thos.	Trapping and Driving	$91.78
McGill, Pat		$80.34
Wilson, James		$50.61
Love, Frank		$68.34
Freemont, James		$51.72
Brown, Geo.		$95.91
Smith, Anthony		$41.19
Muck, Solomon	Watching	$42.69
Erikson, August		$3.06
Peterson, Unnamed		$3.06
Hockingson, John		$6.63
Lawson, John		$6.63
Cook, Edward		$58.92
Hoover, Sam'l		$65.52
Buchanan, Geo.		$58.14
Nelson, Chas. & Son		$111.90
McCollough, H.	Watching	$82.47
Logan, J.W. and Co.	Watching	$103.50

LeeAnn Simmers Dickey

Larson, J.P. & Son		$18.21
Oval, John		$33.18
Bradley, Frank		$15.03
Henry, Joseph		$43.14
Williams, Ed C.		$74.91
Barnett, James		$49.05
Penman, George		$49.05
Lewis, D.R.		$60.42
Harney, Wm. and Co.		$34.65
Davis, John T.		$57.03
Jenkins, Wm. and Co.		$124.89
Johns, Henry		$67.56
Cleave, William		$50.70
Hobbs, Morris and Co.		$66.06
Orpin, John and Co.		$44.43
Williams, E.D.		$.36
Thomas, Thomas		$.36
Crews, William		$45.18
Lynes, John	Uniform rtf	$31.91
Jeffries, Jethro		$22.50
Tilley, John		$22.50
Manifold, George		$23.27
Griffin, John		$88.05
Cubit, John		$88.05
Crowe, Edward	Driving	$11.81
Belger, F.M.	Dumping Coal	$28.87
Jones, John B.	Driving	$49.50
Cribberley, John	Watching and Dumping	$2.37
Lindsay, Charley	Watching and Dumping	$43.93
Gibson, Geo.	Watching and Dumping	$45.25
McCabe, Robert	Watching and Chunking	$48.12
Sparks, O.D.	Watching and Chunking	$43.25
Brown, James	Watching and Dumping	$15.50
Gibson, Harmon	Trapping and Nut Coal Car	$21.13
Mangle, John	Roadman	$1.12
Jones, J.W.	Foreman outside No.1	$66.75
Burdess, Joseph	Engineer	$75.00
Little, Charley	Pumping Engine	$20.00

Before Buxton: The Muchakinock Years

Phillips, Charley	Watching Engine	$40.00
Chilton, Joseph	Pit Boss	$83.33
Phillips, Benj.	Night Watching	$65.00
Sullivan, Con	Conductor	$50.00
Carney, Mike	Roadman	$52.00
Pollock, Hugh	Watching	$2.00
Gibson, S.J.	Tending Mules	$102.00
Evans, Edward	Watching	$1.75
Strickland, Chas.	Watching	$10.50
Butler, W.H.	Watching	$1.50
Ricketts, Shadrick	Watching Pump Engine	$35.00
Paterson, Joseph	Watching	$17.50
Whitsell, H.D.	Repairing Cars	$17.50
Jones, Enezer	Driving	$50.06
Williams, John J.	Driving	$49.50
McCabe, James	Driving	$56.81
Hassey, Thomas	Driving	$34.12
Manger, John	Driving	$52.31
Barnett, Frank	Ties, Props & Caps	$35.69
Chilton, Wm. P.	Ties	$15.62
Acton, William	Caps	$30.83
Heki, Benjamin	Caps	$2.25
Barnett, L.H.	Props	$22.75
Crosson, O.J.	Ties and Props	$224.31
Leggett, John	Car Lumber and Tracking	$57.44
Rowe, L.A.	Elm car planking	$10.33
Willard, Dock	Boss Drivers	$71.25
Ellis, Alonzo	Trapping	$5.10
Davis, Jason	Trapping	$16.36
Loftus, John	Roadman	$65.25
Jones, Johnson	Carpenter	$24.44
Thomas, James	Mining	$16.30
Randolph, A.	Mining	$16.30
Coleman, Thornton	Mining	$16.30
Pendelton, Carter	Mining	$16.30
Berger, David	Mining	$16.30
Carter, Allen	Mining	$16.30
Scott, Benjamin	Mining	$16.30
Carter, Benjamin	Mining	$16.30

LeeAnn Simmers Dickey

Hubbard, Pleasants	Moving Slate	$16.90
Johnson, Houston	Moving Slate	$11.11
Ray, Wm.	Moving Slate	$16.30
Davis, Jefferson	Moving Slate	$16.30
Walker, Charley	Moving Slate	$16.30
Pondexter, Anderson	Moving Slate	$16.30
Harris, Brook	Moving Slate	$16.30
Brookins, Isaac	Moving Slate	$16.30
Carter. Robert	Moving Slate	$16.30
Jones, Charley	Moving Slate	$16.30
Brown, Thomas	Moving Slate	$16.30
Weaver, Elijah	Moving Slate	$16.30
Harris, Simeon	Moving Slate	$16.30
Loving, Adam	Moving Slate	$16.30
Harris, John	Laying Track	$17.30
Dillard, Geo.	Laying Track	$16.30
Mills, Edward	Laying Track	$16.30
Clark, Anthony	Mining	$16.30
Nickson, Thomas	Mining	$16.30
Weathers, James	Mining	$11.11
Jones, Sandy	Mining	$16.30
Myers, Robert	Mining	$16.30
Ragland, John	Mining	$16.30
Chilers, Jake	Mining	$16.30
Williams, Nick	Mining	$16.30
Osbourne, John	Mining	$16.30
Pondexter, Simon	Mining	$16.30
Harvey, Frank	Mining	$16.30
Cox, T.W.	Mining	$16.30
White, Elias	Mining	$16.30
Carter, James	Mining	$16.30
Harris, David	Mining	$8.15
Roy, Philip	Mining	$8.15
Reed, Joseph	Driving	$12.22
Coleman, Mansfield	Nut and Slack	$12.22
Winston, Newton	Driving	$16.30
Harris, William	Driving	$16.30
Davis, William	Driving	$16.30

Before Buxton: The Muchakinock Years

Scott, Henry	Trapping	$8.15
Johnson, Jessie	Trapping	$8.15
Mitchell, James	Trapping	$8.15
Jefferson, J.H.	Trapping	$8.15
Hunter, Wesley		$28.18
Jones, J.T.	Laying Track	$39.92
Brooker, David		$30.92
Walker, Lewis		$29.96
Dyer, Walker		$26.96
Crosby, Walter		$25.36
Bradley, William		$14.60
Bailey, William	Driving	$20.78
Johnson, Chas.	Clearing Roads	$11.00
Gallagher, Wm.	Nut and Slack	$1.72
Reeson, Albert	Chunking	$14.95
Gunsaulis, John	Watching and Driving	$33.40
Beasor, Albert	Driving	$24.15
Bailey, James	Driving and work on tracks	$25.90
Ashman, Sam.	Driving	$23.00
Armstrong, H.A.	Contractor	$114.75
Jones, J.W.	Hauling coal, lumber, brick	$15.00
Muck, Humphry	Watching	$4.50
Barnett, James	Watching	$13.50
Hendricks, A.L.	Watching	$12.00
Marquette, Henry	Load Coal and Watching	$23.75
Love, Frank	Watching	$1.50
Little, Charley	Running pump engine	$20.00
Tilley, William	Fencing Lumber	$2.00
Williams, J.M.	Lumber in Shanty	$6.00
Brown, James	Loading Coal and Watching	$23.75
Burdess, William	Repairing Pump	$3.12
Whitesell, H.D.	Working on Pump	$4.00
Lindsay, Charley	Working on Pump	$.87
McCabe, James	Watching	$1.50
McCabe, Wm.	Watching	$45.00
Brewer, Webster	Ties	$12.93
Heki, Benjamin	Caps	$12.79
Heki, James	Caps	$12.26

LeeAnn Simmers Dickey

Acton, William	Caps	$10.80
Leggett, John	Tracking	$21.00
Mobbley, John	Ties	$1.82
Nash, John W.	Watching and Weighing	$70.00
Gladwin, Ed.	Watching	$16.00
Hobbs, Morris	Watching	$4.00
Muck, Soloman	Watching	$4.00
Muck, Humphry	Training the Blacks	$55.50
Harney, Wm.	Training the Blacks	$63.00
Orpin, John M.	Training the Blacks	$60.00
Evans, Edward	Training the Blacks	$13.00
Bradley, C.F.	Training the Blacks	$42.00
Penman, Alex	Training the Blacks	$3.00
Copple, William	Blacksmith	$40.00
Baxter, Jack	Pit Boss and use of team	$68.00
Newton, Henry	Sinking Shafts- No. 3, 9, & 195	$260.79
Quarls, Baxter	Cook	$12.22
Tyler, Churchman	Cook	$12.22

These payroll records were for Mines No. 1 and No. 3 combined. Out of the 238 workers listed in this month payroll, 40 came out with a zero net income. Some of these workers were paid by the bushel and some were on a $20.00 a month scale. Even with the monthly scale they were only paid for the number of days worked, which equaled around 65 cents per day.

The total output of coal for both mines was 231, 210 bushels. Total Gross Income was $9,351.49. Total Net Income was $5,243.54. Total Debit was $4, 107.92. There were 59 miners that paid the monthly 50 cents insurance.

Before Buxton: The Muchakinock Years

Payroll records for Consolidation Coal Company May 1880

Bosley, Benjamin	Driving	$6.00
Davis, Samuel	Driving	$5.02
Chamber, F. & Son		$5.65
Penman, Alex		$70.32
Johns, Henry		$70.32
Blackstone, John		$6.02
Lewis, John J.		$2.77
Thomas, Thomas		$2.77
Calson, Alex.		$2.40
Quist, Andrew		$2.40
Woskie, P.F.		$3.37
Williams, J.G. & Son		$3.42
McLaughlin, Neal		$7.42
Weese, Elisha		$5.10
Roberts, Lewis		$9.20
Wilson, Park C.		$5.05
Dahn, John		$3.55
Oleson, John		$3.55
Bulger, John	Trapping	$1.36
Johnson, William		$1.82
Swanson, Nelson		$1.82
McMahn, Pat.	Trapping	$4.61
Nicholson, Dorn		$1.87
Williams, John J.	Driving	$6.75
Jones, Wm. J.		$2.80
Roberts, Edwin		$3.57
Oleson, Miles		$1.07
Mobbley, Lon		$3.50
Carney, Thomas		$3.35
Dewey, John		$3.35
Jones, Enezer	Driving and Clearing Track	$6.95

LeeAnn Simmers Dickey

Buchanan, George		$3.90
Cherrington, Wm.	Driving	$4.72
Mobley, R. & Brother		$5.12
Barnett, James		$3.60
Rogers, Jack		$.63
Anderson, A.		$17.67
Dane, Adam		$3.05
Lawson, John		$3.05
Dolphus, Edwin		$6.45
Leaf, Oloff		$10.45
Morris, Morris		$5.80
Anderson, N.		$2.42
Knight, David		$3.80
Anderson, Elias		$1.87
Samuelson, Gus.		$1.87
Anderson, Chas. & Son		$1.02
Terry, John		$.52
Grose, Thomas		$50.07
Bloomfield, Chas.		$50.07
Cadel, John		$5.72
Samuelson, A.		$2.72
McGill, Pat		$2.80
Wright, Thomas	Trapping	$3.36
Orr, John & Son		$5.00
Mobbley, James		$4.62
Freemont, James		$2.05
Erikson, August (John)		$8.45
Samuelson, L.P.		$5.45
Hockingson, John		$4.60
Hoover, Samuel		$10.70
Nelson, Chas. & Son		$4.77
McCollough, H.		$.75
Chilton, Abram		$64.15
Logan, John W.		$64.15
Larson, J & Son		$2.77
Oval, John		$9.87
Williams, Ed C.		$8.40
Penman, George		$6.25

Before Buxton: The Muchakinock Years

Lewis, David R.		$1.85
Marguett, Henry		$5.27
Davis, John T.		$5.07
Jenkins, Wm.		$6.77
Van Cleve, Wm.		$79.98
Creus, William		$4.50
Manger, John	Driving	$.50
Earny, Pink	Chopping Wood	$1.50
Anderson, John	Sawing Rollers and Dumping	$6.75
Fritz, T.O.	Sawing Rollers and Dumping	$6.37
Gibson, George	Dumping	$2.50
Gibson, Harmon	Nut coal car	$2.63
Gibson, S.J.	Tending Mules and Hauling	$31.62
Smith, Adelbert	Dumping	$4.13
Phillips, Ben	Weighing Coal	$6.00
Williams, Ed O.	Building Crib	$1.00
Burdess, Joseph	Engineer	$75.00
Little, Charley	Run Pumping Engine	$20.00
Chilton, Joseph	Pit Boss	$83.33
Willard, Doc	Switching Coal	$50.00
Sullivan, Con	Roadman	$49.00
Carney, Mike	Timbering Rooms	$52.00
McCabe, James	Driving	$2.00
Hassey, Thomas	Driving Mules	$3.43
Davis, Jason	Trapping	$.75
Morris, Wash.	Trapping	$.75
Ellis, Alonzo	Trapping	$.19
Barnett, Frank	Caps @ 1 cent	$7.50
Crosson and Smith	Props @ 6 ½ cents	$2.92
Jones, J.W.	Hauling Wood and Dumping	$15.75
Patterson, Joseph	Watching No.1 Engine	$35.00
Whitesell, Hiram	Carpenter on cars	$3.50
Ricketts, Shadrick	Watching	$30.00

Miners at Buxton, in Monroe County. Consolidation Coal Company moved the operation and workers from Muchakinock to Buxton in about 1900. (Courtesy of Robert Thompson)

These payroll records are for Mine No. 1 at Muchakinock. The miners were paid 2 ½ to 3 cents a bushel for their work. The lowest amount of bushels put out was 25 and the largest was 1,733.

Most of the men here with an occupation listed were paid by the day. Trapping made 75 cents per day. Driving, weighing coal, building crib, roadman, timbering rooms, clearing track, carpenters were paid $2.00 per day. Chopping wood, sawing roller, dumping, hauling slack were paid $1.50 per day.

The amounts listed in these records are the gross pay amounts. Deductions taken out of the gross pay included orders from the store, board bills (such as donations for the band and dances), rent, oil, blacksmith, laundry, fuel, and railway fares and cash advances. Only one of the miners paid the monthly 50 cents charge for insurance.

Out of the 102 miners working in Mine 1 for this month, 46 of them came out at zero net income at the end of the month. The output of coal for this mine in May was 20,504 bushels. Total Gross Income for the miners was $1,248.39. Total Income for the workers was $747.31. Total Debits equaled $501.08.

Before Buxton: The Muchakinock Years

Payroll Records for Consolidation Coal Company
May 1880

Bates, J.H.		$29.03
Slaughter, Mack		$29.04
Carter, Allen	Ditch and Dump	$13.33
Price, Richard	Ditch and Dump	$18.07
Davis, Jefferson	Driving and Trapping	$15.25
Qualls, Baxter		$12.12
Harris, Simon	Work on ditch	$22.08
Carter, Robert	Ditch and Dump	$14.17
Jones, Charlie	Driving and Dump	$15.57
Myers, Robert	Ditch and Dump	$15.68
Kelly, Walter	Waiting on sick and Ditch	$11.20
Brown, Thomas	Ditch and Dump	$20.31
Reevley, Elijah	Ditch and Dump	$18.03
Cox, Tom W.	Ditch and Dump	$20.38
Brown, Robt. S.	Ditch and Dump	$17.20
Roy, Philip	Nut Coal, Ditch and Dump	$20.10
Roy, William	Driving, Ditch and Dump	$19.12
Harris, William	Ditch and Dump, Moving slate	$14.98
Dickerson, Alex.	Work on ditch	$14.98
Johnson, Houston	Work on ditch	$12.11
Southall, Alex.	Work on ditch	$13.75
Randolph, A.	Grading Dump	$19.40
Smith, Nick	Ditch and Dump	$20.40
Miner, Edwin	Ditch and Moving Slate	$19.77
Chillers, Jake		$10.22
Ragland, John	Digging Ditch	$9.35
Weathers, Joe		$.77
Harris, Brooks	Driving and Ditch	$13.53

LeeAnn Simmers Dickey

Johnson, Ned	Work on ditch	$17.12
Harris, John		$2.61
Dillard, Geo.	Driving and Ditch	$22.34
Lee, Hugh	Work on dump	$17.18
Dyer, Walker	Work on dump	$16.80
Campbell, David	Work on ditch	$17.39
Harney, William	Cleaning Track	$41.62
Nelson, Chas.		$43.92
Pondexter, A.	Loading Nut Coal and Dump	$27.22
Walker, Chas.	Nut Coal and Dump	$18.07
Booker, David		$1.11
Walker, Frank	Driving	$16.81
Carter, Ben.	Nut Coal and Grading Dump	$17.86
Cosby, Walter		$20.25
Nixon, Thomas		$3.57
Garrison, Chas.		$6.17
Clark, Anthony	Cleaning Track	$24.06
Mills, Edward	Clearing Track	$27.88
Crank, Bennett	Work on dump	$19.23
Carry, Wilson	Work on dump	$15.44
White, Ellis	Work on dump	$16.37
Brookins, Isaac	Ditch and Dump	$17.47
Henry, Joe	Blowing down roof	$37.57
Dumont, Geo.	Blowing down roof	$37.57
Wignall, James		$59.32
Lewis, Di. J.		$5.25
Maupin, Sam		$5.26
Turner, Andy		$9.48
Harris, Charlie	Work on ditch	$18.85
Brown, Washington	Cleaning wells	$18.05
Allens, Charlie	Ditch and Dump	$18.23
Karr, John	Ditch and Dump	$69.05
Stanton, James	Cleaning Track	$65.62
Northway, Mose		$19.25
Caul, G.S.	Work on dump	$19.63
Thomas, W.S.	Work on dump	$16.87
Garlane, Andrew	Work on ditch	$16.11

Before Buxton: The Muchakinock Years

McKinney, Jasper	Work on ditch	$17.61
Koiner, F.P.	Grading Dump	$16.47
Southall, William	Work on dump	$15.56
Lindsay, Chas.	Grading Dump	$14.80
Koiner, Burt	Work on dump	$14.96
Willis, Sam.	Work on ditch	$30.28
Carter, Fitz		$23.29
Woodforth, Ben.		$14.98
Scott, Hillery	Works on scales	$15.32
Copeland, Isaac	Digging Ditch	$17.70
Hughes, Henry	Work on ditch	$16.73
Walker, Lewis		$27.80
Mayes, W.S.		$30.10
Green, John	Work on grade	$19.38
Sheffy, John	Work on ditch	$21.31
Brown, Dave	Moving Slate and Ditch	$5.39
Carter, James	Digging Ditches	$16.92
Givins, Mose	Ditch and Dump, Grading	$14.29
Jones, Sandy	Ditch and Dump	$26.67
Hockingson, John		$26.67
Larson, John P.		$26.67
Dane, Adam		$26.67
Dolphus, Edwin		$26.67
Roberts, Leon	Work on pit mouth	$24.28
Franklin, Sam.	Work on pit mouth	$23.89
Lewis, Henry		$5.36
Carroll, Jessie		$5.35
Bush, Frank	Loading Nut Coal	$21.90
Leftwich, Payton	Work on dump	$18.29
Smith, Anthony	Work in rooms	$11.61
Buchner, Lewis	Work on ditch	$12.30
Robinson, Lindsay		$7.68
Carry, James	Work on grade	$8.09
Martin, James	Work on wells and driving	$8.25
Lewis, George	Work on pit mouth	$2.41
Howard, Wm.	Slack and Nut	$6.80

LeeAnn Simmers Dickey

Coleman, Thornton & Son	Work on ditch	$28.62
Gibson, S.J.	Hauling for No.3 engine	$24.00
Anderson, John	Quarry Rock, Rollers, Grading	$25.12
Fritz, T.O.	Ditching and Grading	$22.12
Gibson, George	Ditching and Grading	$19.12
Jones, Enezer	Driving and Scales	$25.87
Smith, Adelbert	Ditching and Grading	$12.37
Phillips, Charley	Work on No. 3 engine	$39.00
McNeill, Frank	Hauling Lumber	$10.50
Phillips, Ben.	Making rollers	$45.00
Erikson, August	Cutting up boiler iron	$1.50
Barnett, James	Hauling Lumber and stone	$15.75
Williams, J.G.	Ditching and Grading	$13.50
Nicholson, Dorn	Scales and Ditching	$19.00
Johnson, Sam	Work on engine	$6.75
Samuelson, N.G.	Work on engine	$6.75
Samuelson, A.	Work on engine	$6.75
Samuelson, L.P.	Scales, Ditch and Dump	$4.50
Butler, William	Work on scale pit	$5.25
McCollough, Harvey	Scale, Ditch and Dump	$5.62
Anderson, C.	Work on Co. houses	$9.75
Swanson, Nelson	Work on Co. houses	$6.37
Little, Charlie	Run pump engine	$20.00
Burdess, William	Work on engine pit	$55.00
Dahn, John	Carpenter work	$6.00
Whitsell, Hiram	Carpenter work on houses	$35.00
Jones, J.W.	Ditch, Dump and Hauling	$111.75
Oleson, John	Work on houses	$18.37
McCabe, Wm.	Watching No. 3 dump	$35.00
Orpin, John	Schooling Blacks	$45.00
Muck, Humphry	Instructing Blacks	$47.00
Titus, Wm. D.	Instructing Blacks	$38.00
Jones, Johnson	Roadman	$22.62
Farrer, Henry	Work on dump and houses	$21.16
Muck, Solomon	Instructing Blacks	$21.00
Wilson, P.C.	Instructing Blacks	$27.00
Gunsaulis, John	Nut Coal, Slate and Driving	$30.37

Before Buxton: The Muchakinock Years

Cross, Wm. T.	Blacksmithing	$25.38
Davis, William	Driving, Slate and Carpentry	$22.36
Gibbins, Estial	Timbering and Carpenter	$20.77
Reed, Ned.	Cleaning Track	$7.70
Evans, Edward	Trapping	$4.12
Scott, Benj.	Driving and Moving Gob	$21.59
Blackstone, Jeff	Timber @ $1.00 per 100 ft.	$20.93
Leggett, Edward	2,901 ft. track @$2.10	$60.92
Crosson and Smith	Ties, Props and Timbers	$63.39
Barnett, Frank	1,690 caps @ 1 cent	$16.90
Barnett, L.H.	580 caps @ 1 cent	$5.80
Nash, John W.	Weighing Coal	$52.00
Copple, William	Blacksmith	$50.00
Baxter, Jack	Pit Boss	$75.00
Woods, James	Ditch and Dump	$18.09
Lewis, Chris	Ditch and Dump	$3.85
Beason, Albert	Driving	$30.63
Pendelton, Carter	Nut Coal and Driving	$20.82
Evans, Joseph	Driving	$23.08
Winston, Newton	Driving	$20.00
Garlane, Jackson	Driving	$13.47
Sheffey, John P.	Nut Coal and Driving	$24.79
Hill, R.T.	Driving	$20.00
Hogsett, Robt.	Nut Coal and Driving	$20.50
Reesor, John	Nut Coal and Chunking	$30.54
Pollock, Hugh	Nut Coal and Chunking	$25.65
Irvin, Page	Nut Coal and Slack	$21.77
Smith, Saml.	Nut Coal and Slack	$20.50
Loving, Adam	Nut Coal and Driving	$20.83
Foster, J.L.	Painting	$18.46
Edmonds, John	Painting	$18.46
Irvin, Mary	Cooking	$8.00
Bess, Julia	Cooking	$8.00
Carter, Annie	Cooking	$8.00
Maupin, Grace	Cooking	$8.00
Bates, Mary	Cooking	$8.00
Garrison, Mimie	Cooking	$8.00

Overall view of Buxton, where many of the houses from Muchakinock were moved when Consolidation Coal Company shifted their mining operations to Monroe County. Date not known. (Lee Ann Simmers Dickey)

Robinson, Mary	Cooking	$8.00
Howard, Retta	Cooking	$10.00
Coleman, Mary	Cooking	$10.00
Mayes, Annie	Cooking	$10.00
Woodfork, Lizzie	Cooking	$10.00
Jefferson, Cornelia	Cooking	$10.00
Sheffy, Eliza	Cooking	$10.00
Sheffy, Margaret	Cooking	$10.00
Armstrong, H.A.	Hired Mules and Feed	$169.55
Churchman, Tyler	Cooking	$20.00

Before Buxton: The Muchakinock Years

Strikebreakers Recruited

Thomas Shumate was hired to recruit African-Americans from Virginia in 1880 as strikebreakers. Handbills were put up in likely towns, and usually a man was hired to hand out handbills that included the place to meet Shumate if willing to work. The first of the recruits arrived in Muchakinock on March 5, 1880. Most members of the first group were recruited from Staunton and Charlottesville, with two from Fluvanna County, four from Lynchville and two who joined on in Cincinnati, Ohio. There was one woman in this group, along with about 65 men, but no children.

Individuals arriving in the first group included: Ellis White, William J. Jones, Brooks Harris, Arminius Randolph, Randolph Willis, Washington Matthews, Taylor Jefferson, Thornton A. Coleman, Daniel Harris, Frances Briggs (the only female), Daniel Booker (he left before second group), Lee Bugher (left soon after), Isaac Brooken (he got sick and left), Thomas Cox, Simon Bowles, William Harris, Joseph Anderson, Arthur Jackson, James Miner, and Charles Pillson.

The second recruiting trip was made in April 4, 1880, and resulted in about 70 people coming to Muchakinock. The group included women and children. Thomas (Major) Shumate was acquainted with the second lot as they were from his hometown.

Individuals arriving in the second group included: R. T. Hall, Page Irwin, Chris Lewis, Sam Willis, Joyce Kenny, Robert F. Hogsett, Ruben Hill, Washington Brown, John P. Sheffey, David J. Campbell, Geo. S. Caul, Wilson Cary, William T. Cross, Jasper Kenny, Christopher Lewis, Charles Linsey, Sam Willis, J. L. Foster, J. L. Edwards, Austin Gibbs, Burnett Crank, Dol Lamar, Alex Dickerson, Hillary Scott, Burt Barnard, Charles Allen, Frank Bush, John Carr.

The third group of recruits left Staunton, Virginia on May 12, 1880 and arrived in Muchakinock on May 15, 1880. There were about 50 in this group, with a good number of families included in the total. On the trip from Marshalltown to Muchakinock, the No. 4 passenger car they rode in was called "The Black Maria," a name given to it by the railroad employees. It was located at the end of freight train No. 6. The conductor was Charles E. Smith. Muchakinock was Station No. 152.

Individuals arriving in the third group included: Jesse Carroll, George Washington Lewis, Wm. T. Howard, Henry Lewis, James S. Martin, Charlie Garrison, James Cary, Lindsa Robinson, William Southall, Andrew Turner, James H. Bates, Samuel Moppin, Hardin White, Sarah (Sophie) Foster — wife of J. L. Foster.

LeeAnn Simmers Dickey

Lindsa Robinson is one who could read and write and he made the trip to be the leader of the Muchakinock Band.

The fourth group of recruits arrived on July 1, 1880. The rail fare from Virginia to Iowa was twelve dollars, and the amount was withheld from each miner's first wages. Most of the men that were recruited brought their entire families along. Working in the coal mines allowed them to make a decent wage and support their families. The men received their pay the 20th day of each month.

W.J. Jones, C.R. Foster and Hobart Armstrong also traveled to Virginia to recruit workers. Six different trips had been made by October 6, 1882. All the trips but one took the Chesapeake and Ohio route from Virginia to Cincinnati and then to Chicago on the Indianapolis, Cincinnati and Lafayette Railroad. Then from Chicago to Marshalltown, they took the Chicago and Northwestern train. The Iowa Central Railroad then brought the groups to Muchakinock.

The third lot came by the Baltimore and Ohio road as far as Chicago and then the same route as the other groups. It was a twelve to fourteen hour trip and would get them to Muchakinock in a day. Taylor Jefferson was the first recruit to send back to Virginia for his family. Most of the miners went to work in Mine 3. Charles F. Little was the nephew of the McNeil brothers. He operated the pump house for Mine No. 3. When they arrived on the trains they went to the diner on the hill to eat. It was named the Bee Hive. The Bee Hive burned in September of 1887.

Individuals arriving in the fourth

Anderson Perkins, postmaster
(Courtesy of Traci Davis)

Before Buxton: The Muchakinock Years

group included: Adam Fielding, W. S. Thoms, Sophy Banks, James Usher, John Clark, William Garland, Spence James, John W. Jackson, Ernest Linsey, G. W. Randel, James Ash, Hesekiah Adams, Rev. Charles Brookens, wife of Frank Bush.

John Hawkins arrived on September 27, 1880 along with Joseph James.

The fifth group of recruits arrived October 28, 1880 and consisted of three carloads of mostly men.

Individuals arriving in the fifth group included: Minor Henderson, Tom Brown, Titus Cosby, Harry Irwin, Henry Jones, Isaac Downey, James Byers, William H. Hues, Sam Winbush, Randolph Willis

Albert Chapman also arrived in October of 1880 from Charlottesville, Virginia. Major Shumate deducted $23.15 from Chapman's pay for bringing his wife and two children. Chapman complained that Shumate overcharged him and was reimbursed $13.00 by the company.

Addison Rhodes was from Staunton, Virginia and had worked for Major Shumate in 1874. He came to Iowa January 14, 1881 and became one of the leaders for the African American colony in Muchakinock.

Samuel Watkins arrived in September of 1881.

Andrew Lewis and Edward Willis arrived in October of 1881.

A sixth group of recruits was brought to Muchakinock but the date of their arrival in Iowa is not known. Those in the sixth group included: Alexander Burkes, Chas. Spinner, Moses Strother, Robert. Allen, David Marshall, Henry Jones, Berkeley Reed, Sam Bryan, Nelson, Woodford, Hillary Scott, James Osten, David Harris, Dennis Harris, Walker Dyer.

In 1882 some of these miners left Consolidation Coal Company and went to work for Excelsior Mines. Mr. Ramsey was the superintendent there, and the general manager of Excelsior Mines was Mr. Whitman. Miners who left were: Simon Bowles, Dwight F. Downing, James Miner, Jasper Kinney, William Harris, David Marshall, John Carr, Joseph Anderson, Thomas Cox, Henry Jones, Ellis White, Alexander Burkes, and J. L. Foster. Foster's wife also went and ran a boarding house.

In 1887 the miners established the Mutual Protection Society, one of the first insurance protections in Iowa. A single miner paid fifty cents per month, and the cost of family protection was one dollar per month. Eighty percent of the monthly cost went for health insurance. The remainder went into a fund for members' burial

LeeAnn Simmers Dickey

Rebecca Nichols Perkins
(Courtesy of Traci Davis)

---

expenses. If the miner was hurt or sick, he could receive three dollars a week during his illness.

In 1894 the Bituminous Coal Miners' Strike lasted from April to May. All of Iowa's Coal Mines went on strike, except for Muchakinock and Evans Mines. After being a non-union camp for more than twenty years in September of 1900, Muchakinock became a union camp. Muchakinock had always been non-union and had always avoided the men striking. In September 1900, in order to avoid trouble, Superintendent Buxton convinced the miners to join the union. The United Mine Workers of America organized a camp with 255 charter members; at least half of the workers were African-American. The non-union miners at Muchakinock actually made more money than workers at the union camps, so they could lose some of their wages by joining the union. However, Consolidation Coal chose not to cut back on the union members' wages.

Before Buxton: The Muchakinock Years

Miners killed in Accidents in the Mines at Muchakinock

Robert Hughes, aged 35, was killed in Mine No. 1 on November 20, 1879, due to fall of slate.

Cliff Thompson, son of Lee Thompson, was killed in Mine No. 1 on February 9, 1883, due to fall of slate.

Mr. Leif, a Swede, was killed in Mine No. 1 on January 16, 1884, due to fall of slate.

William Dorsey, aged 38, was killed in Mine No. 5 on March 27, 1885, due to fall of slate.

A.M. Peterson, was killed in Mine No. 5 on December 19, 1885, due to explosion.

Charles Sequest, a Swede, was killed in Mine No. 5 on October 25, 1886, due to fall of slate.

C.A. Nelson was killed on September 22, 1897, due to injuries received in Mine No. 8.

Ed Dolphus, a Swede, was killed in Mine No. 5 on December 21, 1887, due to explosion.

William Lewis, colored, was killed in Mine No. 8 on July 14, 1898, due to fall of slate.

Willis Turner, was killed in Mine No. 8 on November 21, 1900, due to "a windy shot". (A windy shot is when the powder in place does not explode and tear down the coal, but flies back in the room, igniting the dust and causing an explosion.)

Elmer Moore was killed instantly on October 15, 1898, due to falling under the coal cars in Mine No. 9.

Coal Valley/Muchakinock as it looked in 1913

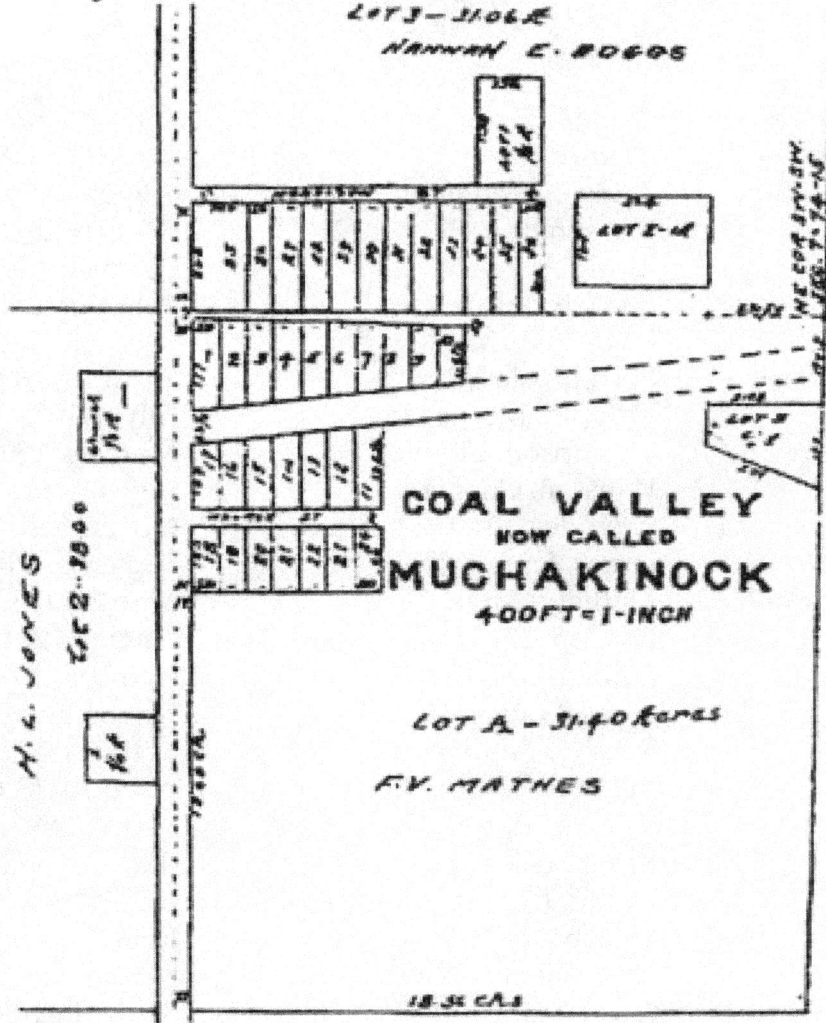

Plat map of Muchakinock in 1913. (Mahaska County plat map books)

Before Buxton: The Muchakinock Years

Mahaska County African American Marriages 1880-1921

Groom's name / age	Bride's name / age	Date of marriage
Adams, Charles 37	Griffin, Nancy 34	January 23, 1888
Adams, Charles 43	Anderson, Florence 25	August 20, 1897
Albert, Vena 27	Washington, Phoeba 25	January 25, 1883
Allen, John 26	McGuire, Mary C.	October 9, 1884
Allen, John H. 34	Bartlow, Altha 19	February 25, 1895
Allen, Nelson 27	Undertree, Mary	September 23, 1885
Allen, Nelson 39	Ford, Jessie 22	April 29, 1899
Allen, William H. 23	Moppin, Mattie 25	July 3, 1883
Anderson, Robert 38	Thompson, Eldora 28	March 4, 1902
Anderson, William E. 22	Winston, Chanie 21	June 8, 1885
Appleton, Victor B. 24	Crowder, Ruth 20	November 17, 1917
Archer, W.H. 39	James, Jennie 23	September 14, 1882
Armstrong, Charles W. 26	Mathew, Anna 21 (W)	May 28, 1889
Arthur, Henry 40	Jackson, Emma	August 12, 1882
Ashby, George 22	Jones, Mary 16	October 1, 1884
Ashby, Howard 25	Jones, Louisa 19	November 28, 1883
Ashby, Howard 28	Reasby, Pauline	May 5, 1889
Atchison, Jasper 31	McClain, Laura M. 19	April 20, 1894
Atkinson, Beveley 23	Dorsey, Mattie 22	May 6, 1886
Atkinson, Beveley 23	Kiney, Alice	(License Only) 1884
Autry, John 30	Harris, Lou 21	July 18, 1883
Avery, L.A. 40	Blackburn, Elizabeth	June 7, 1905
Bailey, John 24	Newman, Fannie 26	November 27, 1881
Baker, John 25	Carey, Lucy	September 24, 1894
Banks, Lewis 23	Hickman, Lucy 20	April 13, 1887
Banks, George 33	Niles, Sophia	December 10, 1891
Barber, Charles E. 26	Tobin, Bertha 20	December 23, 1911
Barber, Rice 23	Brown, Charity 19	December 28, 1885
Barquett, John Pierre 20	Sanford, Ione	(License Only) 1903
Bassett, Israel 22	Duke, Rosella 15	February 21, 1886
Bates, H. Elliott 25	Miller, Carrie 28	May 10, 1902

LeeAnn Simmers Dickey

Groom	Bride	Date
Baxter, John Jr. 32 (W)	Armstrong, Lottie C. 25	February 27, 1901
Bell, Richard 23	Bolden, Mary 18	June 17, 1893
Bell, Richard 28	Marshall, Jennetta 19	October 25, 1898
Bell, William 26	Richardson, Susan 19	June 3, 1895
Bellenfant, H.H. 33	Jefferson, Sallie 19	December 25, 1895
Bennett, C.R.	Contee, Molly 31	October 28, 1885
Black, G.W.	Buckner, Emma B. 27	January 8, 1891
Blackman, Early 23	Walker, Rena 23	March 29, 1887
Blakely, James 31	Minier, Wirginia 26	January 19, 1882
Blakely, John 40	Walker, Eliza 27	February 1898
Blakely, R.D. 29	Burket, Marietta 18	April 1898
Blakey, Simon 38	Tolliver, Mary 25	September 25, 1884
Bledsoe, Ovid L. 31	Cary, Letta E. 29	June 20, 1917
Bolden, Lee 27	Harris, Maud 19	August 3, 1905
Boles, Henry 25	Watkin, Alice 21	January 22, 1889
Boles, Simon 29	Alexander, Ella 19	November 27, 1889
Bolls, Simon 28	Spears, Amy 22	September 22, 1884
Booker, James E. 37	Finks, Lottie 25	September 19, 1891
Boon, Emanuel 22	Harris, Amy 22	February 8, 1882
Bowles, James 22	Bedford, Hostella 19	December 24, 1887
Boyers, J.W. 25	Brown, Effie 20	October 22, 1896
Brackstron, William 33	Harris, Sarah 29	(License Only) 1889
Bradford, Sam 46	Brooks, Daisy Mrs. 32	October 6, 1917
Bradley, Tandy 34	Fry, Elly 24	October 15, 1890
Bragg, Marmion 22	Bohanna, Ida 19	December 6, 1884
Brasco, William L. 47	Morrison, Elizabeth 25	April 20, 1917
Brinker, Charles G. 26	Parker, Julia 23	May 23, 1893
Broddus, John 37	Wilson, Melinda 23	June 30, 1894
Bronaddus, John 24	Franklin, Elizabeth 23	May 3, 1893
Brookins, Isaac 31	Jefferson, Mary J. 37	October 25, 1890
Brooks, David 26	Briggs, Fannie 28	November 11, 1884
Brooks, Charles G. 26	Rhodes, Mattie 18	January 10, 1891
Brooks, Harry 23	Thomas, Mariah 22	October 31, 1891
Brown, Alonzo 44	Hervey, Nellie 25	July 21, 1915
Brown, French 22	Carey, Selina 19	December 25, 1897
Brown, Grant 50	Saunders, Kittie Hill 42	October 10, 1916
Brown, Henry 28	Cooper, Minnie 19	August 28, 1886
Brown, Isaac L. 22	Wilson, Martha 23	November 24, 1882

Before Buxton: The Muchakinock Years

Brown, Jacob Jr. 22	Jones, Fannie 18	January 23, 1893
Brown, Jacob 26	Williams, Hattie L. 26	February 10, 1897
Brown, James 73	Walker, Alice 30	May 28, 1903
Brown, John Henry 37	Starcher, Eliza 37	April 23, 1909
Brown, Luther H.S. 22	Brown, Mary E. 19	(License Only) 1896
Brown, Marshall 31	Straughter, Rachel 17	October 15, 1889
Brown, R.J. 28	Woody, Ida 23	September 7, 1882
Brown, Thomas 45	Givens, Harriet 29	October 31, 1880
Brown, Washington 31	Brown, Hillie 22	December 25, 1886
Brown, Washington 39	Johnson, Nannie 35	(License Only) 1897
Brown, William 54	Braxton, Eveline 38	July 20, 1918
Brown, William 39	Johnson, Gertrude 21	August 31, 1902
Brown, W.M. 45	Kline, Annie A. Waters 33 (W)	August 13, 1901
Brown, W.N. 29	Strange, Rosa	January 21, 1891
Bryant, A. Jr. 23	Scott, Sarah 21	(License Only) 1884
Bryant, Henry 37	Grady, Ada May Price 25	November 28, 1894
Bryant, Norris 40	Manders, Lizzie 22	December 20, 1900
Bryant, Norris 35	Duke, Mattie 25	(License Only) 1903
Bryant, Samuel 29	Cole, Sallie A. 22	June 22, 1893
Bryson, John 24	Hunderson, Hattie 19	November 20, 1913
Bryson, W.E. 23	Garland, Pearle 19	March 13, 1905
Buckner, Dudley 23	Marshall, Julia 20	December 25, 1881
Buckner, L.D. 26	Buckner, Julia 24	(License Only) 1890
Buckner, Grant 22	Cooper, Cora E. 15	July 21, 1887
Buckner, William T. 27	Yieser, Syrilda 30	April 19, 1899
Burgess, William J. 30	Johnson, Pearl Hale 26	December 26, 1896
Burgess, William 70	Sommers, Elsie J. 50	February 2, 1914
Burke, John E. 38	Myers, Sophie Harris 24	June 29, 1889
Burke, John E. 39	Bolden, Susan Harvey 34	June 25, 1890
Burkes, Phillip 23	Carter, Margaret 21	September 30, 1881
Burket, Henry 35	Smith, Dora 38	April 1898
Burket, Phillip 24	Pritchett, Mary 21	April 17, 1903
Burnes, Walter B. 20	Nelson, Virgie 19	January 13, 1888
Burns, Joseph 30	Emery, Lizzie	(License Only) 1885
Burns, Lee 24	Cogan, Cora V. 19	October 13, 1903
Burns, Robert 35	Givin, Amanda 25	January 26, 1888
Burrell, Robert 23	McGee, Lulu 25	October 27, 1905
Burton, Lowell 23	Davis, Della 19	June 26, 1902

LeeAnn Simmers Dickey

Byers, James 26	Lewis, Emma 19	November 4, 1885
Cabbell, J.H. 26	Ford, Anna T. 21	February 2, 1886
Caldwell, Fred 23	Craddock, Enola 19	August 15, 1907
Campbell, Julian J. 33	Killion, Bertah 27	September 25, 1917
Cannaday, John T. 32	Murray, Isabella 20	September 24, 1884
Cannaday, J.T. 38	Johnson, Addie L. 28	December 8, 1890
Carey, P.F. 30	Farrar, Mattie H. 30	May 25, 1893
Carey, Spencer 22	Gordon, Permelia 23	November 8, 1881
Carr, James 23	Scott, Mary 23	December 17, 1887
Carr, James 28	Clark, Mary 17	June 29, 1895
Carr, James Sr. 44	Peaco, Millie 43	January 24, 1916
Carr, John 26	Nicholas, Sophia 27	March 23, 1887
Carter, Davis 29	Foster, Rosa Taylor 19	June 25, 1902
Carter, Elmer 38	Johnson, Margaret 26	November 24, 1917
Carter, Frank 24	Collins, Dora E. 19	September 12, 1888
Carter, Frank 29	Mitchell, Carrie 28 (W)	October 6, 1894
Carter, Frank 29	Mitchell, Carrie Mrs. 28 (W)	May 29, 1895
Carter, J.H. 23	Reasby, Mary 18	July 23, 1888
Carter, John 24	Brown, Iva 21	December 26, 1907
Carter, Oscar 24	Barnes, Ida Mae 16	August 11, 1886
Carter, Oscar 25	Cook, Rosa 20	April 8, 1889
Carter, W.A. 24	Moon, Alice Lewis 24	July 26, 1883
Carey, Lewis C.	Perkins, Bertha 20	October 18, 1899
Cary, Alfoncer 25	Cosby, Lucy 21	October 1, 1889
Cary, Newton R. 23	Leighton, Anna 26	September 2, 1891
Cary, W.W. 26	Walker, Mary A.	February 7, 1884
Cassels, Mark E. 23	Bennett, Lulu 19	January 10, 1904
Caul, George S. 25	Coleman, Annie	August 30, 1883
Chapman, Abraham 23	Brown, Sallie 19	May 31, 1888
Chapman, John 30	James, Willie 25	April 24, 1895
Chaney, Robert 22	Wheeler, Mary E. 16	February 26, 1898
Cheek, T.C. 29	Smith, Etta 28	May 24, 1893
Chockolett, William 28	West, Cornelia 36	June 16, 1915
Christian, John J. 38	Walker, Julia C. Mass	April 12, 1905
Churten, George 45	Gray, Mattie 42	September 9, 1912
Claborn, Phillip 27	Dray, Mary L. 19	March 3, 1886
Clark, Anthony 36	Harris, Alice 25	December 20, 1881
Clark, Lewis 50	Lee, Patsy	November 28, 1895

Before Buxton: The Muchakinock Years

Clark, Lewis 58	Steward, I.L. Mrs. 66	November 17, 1903
Clay, Charles C. 29	Brown, Mary Etta 25	February 8, 1900
Cleaver, Barney 24	Bedford, Stella 22	October 28, 1891
Clements, Thomas 26	Storeall, Lucy Harvey 19	February 1, 1904
Cogbill, W.R. 24	Harvey, Louisa 23	May 4, 1886
Coleman, Charles H. 29	Boyer, Lena	November 27, 1894
Coleman, James 31	Willis, Georgia 22	March 26, 1896
Coleman, Winston C. 39	Sanford, Cassie 22	July 2, 1898
Coles, Charles 40	Kelley, Hannah Lipkins 42	April 22, 1905
Combs, Thomas 25	Marshall, Carrie M. 17	October 26, 1892
Conaway, James 24	Williams, Henrietta 23	February 26, 1895
Conner, Henry 28	Hickman, Gladness 18	November 27, 1897
Connor, J.C. 30	Sanford, Edna 25	December 27, 1904
Cook, W.H. 34	Allen, Phoebe 34	August 23, 1899
Cosby, Titus 22	Brown, Lucy 20	May 3, 1886
Coshey, Robert A. 50	Cowens, Mattie Moore 25	January 13, 1902
Cottons, Walker B. 22	Carter, Ellen 23	September 14, 1895
Cowan, Jesse 22	Moore, Mattie 21	September 30, 1890
Cowan, Richard 56	Hicks, Susan 20	June 9, 1888
Crank, Bennett 27	Harris, Susan 20	February 15, 1887
Crawford, W.D. 28	Wayland, Laura Ross 25	March 25, 1886
Crawley, W.H. 24	Turner, Martha J. 19	August 11, 1894
Crump, Marshall 21	Hart, Ada 20	March 25, 1909
Crump, William J. 23	Barquet, Connie H. 21	May 22, 1907
Crittenden, G.D. 30	Madison, Americus 20	April 28, 1892
Crockett, James 25	Oliver, Callie 20	March 27, 1886
Curry, Leonard 24	Robinson, Bettie 20	May 26, 1898
Dalhay, Lewis 22	Davis, Mildred 19	December 26, 1885
Daniel, William 32	Wilson, Nannie 16	April 11, 1898
Daniels, I.N. 28	Lucas, Emma	April 8, 1886
Daniels, William 27	Finley, Bertha 20	August 8, 1903
Davis, John L. 36	Pritchard, Eliza 45	October 2, 1899
Davis, Robert 29	Jackson, Maude 25	April 19, 1909
Davis, Thos. J. 33	Christmas, Minnie 20	July 9, 1917
Davis, William 26	Murray, Annie 22	September 5, 1880
Davis, William 45	Johnson, Irene 26	July 3, 1916
Davis, William H. 27	Harvey, Mary 20	August 25, 1886
Davis, W.M. 52	Murry, Belle 38	February 10, 1919

LeeAnn Simmers Dickey

Groom	Bride	Date
Dickerson, Alexander 30	Robison, Polly 29	September 25, 1880
Dickerson, Alexander 59	Fields, Jane Mrs. 40	July 13, 1893
Diggs, Roland 28	Patton, Ella 25	March 20, 1893
Diggs, Wesley 34	Brown, Lizzie 19	June 6, 1895
Dillard, George 22	Reed, Amanda 21	July 21, 1880
Dishman, C.A. 42	Waters, Jane 28	April 30, 1906
Donnell, David Jr. 34	Brown, Nancy 38	(License Only) 1884
Dorsey, C.A. 32	Beber, Mary 27	April 22, 1895
Dorsey, Charles 22	Cusin, Alice 19	October 28, 1885
Dougherty, Henry 30	Burns, Lizzie 31	May 4, 1893
Douglas, Richard Jr. 37	Tyler, Kittie Turner 45	August 23, 1892
Douglas, Richard Jr. 39	Jefferson, Hester 22	June 25, 1894
Douglass, John N. 26	Padgett, Cornelia 21	December 27, 1887
Douglass, Robert 23	Steele, Maud 16	April 16, 1901
Dowling, Joseph A. 24	Buckner, Lucy 19	October 27, 1885
Drew, J.R. 24	Cary, Belzora 21	February 15, 1899
Driver, William Arthur 22	Barber, Deborah 20	February 16, 1915
Duke, J.N. 28	Anderson, Annie B. 17	November 28, 1906
Duncan, W.S. 31	Johnson, Ella 23	September 3, 1901
Dunnigan, Geo. Wash. 30	Bartlow, Edna 19 (W)	December 3, 1887
Dyer, Herman W. 33	Ernest, Marguerite 26	May 7, 1918
Dyer, Herman W. 21	Mickle, Izora 19	February 13, 1903
Early, Soine 23	Yates, Kittie 19	November 3, 1887
Earley, William H. 29	Slaughter, Maggie 19	April 3, 1893
Edgar, Wardell 23	Claybourne, Mamie 17	July 19, 1899
Edgar, Walter 24	Mines, Maggie Adams 26	September 20, 1890
Edgar, Walter 29	Banks, Mary 19	September 25, 1890
Edmonds, John L. 23	Carpenter, Rosa A. 19	November 11, 1885
Edmundson, Wm. 25	Wilson, Anna B. 26	January 1, 1890
Edwards, Walter E. 22	Chavis, Dora A.R. 19	July 7, 1885
Ewing, Robert 28	Jones, Lucy 24	April 5, 1890
Fairfax, Phillip C. 27	Baker, Ella 21	October 5, 1885
Farmer, D. 23	Bedford, Stella 20	October 10, 1888
Ferrell, William A. 25	Lay, Minnie 31	January 22, 1901
Fielding, George 27	Brock, Lizzie 20	June 16, 1900
Fielding, Marshall 22	Johnson, Ella 21	February 24, 1896
Fields, Roscoe 24	Davis, Liv 31	April 1, 1908
Fields, Thomas 24	Buckner, Ethel 19	August 26, 1909

Before Buxton: The Muchakinock Years

Findley, Cyrus 30	Green, Mable 25	June 5, 1912
Fleming, William 22	Carter, Ida Barnes 19	February 21, 1888
Floyd, George William 33	Jefferson, Emma 22	February 23, 1903
Ford, Eugene 22	Thompson, Ida 19	(License Only) 1891
Foster, Charley L. 32	Smith, Anna 26	February 28, 1907
Foster, James L. 36	Hurtt, Mary J. 23	March 14, 1894
Fox, Thomas 38	Johnson, Jennie 23	November 18, 1896
Franklin, Harry 22	Green, Annie 18	January 19, 1902
Franklin, Kinney S. 24	Bates, Laura 19	June 27, 1889
Franklin, Samuel 24	Clock, Elsie 22	October 18, 1882
Frazier, G.W. 30	Bassett, Dora M. 23	October 22, 1891
Frazier, W.R. 23	Bickley, Sarah F. 20	January 24, 1890
Freeman, George 22	Miller, Elizabeth 23	March 31, 1886
Gaines, Harry 26	Thompsom., Betty 22	October 18, 1882
Gaines, Leonard 22	Jackson, Maude 18	September 6, 1900
Gallant, James 22	Hale, Ora M. 22	November 19, 1912
Gambles, Sam 35	Williams, Tisha 24	July 28, 1897
Gant, James 27	Williams, Louisa 23	June 13, 1881
Garland, Andrew 22	Thompson, Mary S. 21	August 21, 1881
Garland, Ellis 22	Jackson, Mollie 24	October 12, 1886
Garland, Jackson 25	Reeser, Julia M.	September 5, 1882
Garland, Lewis A. 20	Bowman, Jessie 19	October 4, 1906
Garland, Thomas A. 24	Madison, Eva 27	February 15, 1886
Garland, William 24	Reasby, Julia 21	April 6, 1883
Gibbons, T.J. 23	Harris, Laura A. 19	September 6, 1882
Gibbons, William M. 26	Gordon, Nettie 19	March 24, 1917
Gibson, Lewis 28	Strowther, Maggie 18	December 24, 1884
Gibson, Lewis 45	Carson, Eliza Lewis 40	October 3, 1900
Gillett, C.A. 23	Woodfork, Julia E. 21	January 29, 1890
Gilmore, Wm. 32	McGuffey, Annie 27	December 24, 1881
Goggins, F.H. 28	Brown, Lucy 18	December 24, 1891
Goings, George 24	Tolliver, Rhoda 23	November 1, 1888
Goode, E. 28	Craige, Anna 21	May 3, 1887
Graham, James A. 32	Hoyl, Hattie 33	March 21, 1903
Graham, John 28	Nelson, Harriet 23	(License Only) 1901
Granderson, Meredith 37	Young, Caroline	December 1, 1890
Grant, Fred 29	Watkins, Florence 28	June 2, 1908
Graves, Anderson 30	Dickason, Nannoe 20	(License Only) 1886

LeeAnn Simmers Dickey

Graves, Daniel 22	Bagby, Lee 19	December 23, 1907
Graves, Hampton 27	Brown, Fannie E. Jones 21	November 5, 1895
Gravitt, Richard 68	Burgess, Alisey 66	April 26, 1921
Green, Arthur 22	Molure, Ada 21	February 6, 1902
Green, Callis 27	Johnson, Fannie 23	April 26, 1888
Green, Henry 48	Tiffin, Jennie B. 40	January 25, 1910
Green, William L. 25	Rhodes, Selena 20	December 4, 1899
Gregg, George 23	Tyler, Nannie 19	(License Only) 1892
Griffin, Otis 25	Willis, Georgiana 17	April 22, 1890
Griffin, Pearl 24	Harris, Hazel 20	September 7, 1909
Grimes, James 26	Harris, Maggie 19	July 3, 1894
Guy, Jimmie 22	Lewis, Agnes 19	June 11, 1907
Hackley, Robert 38	Wright, Sarah A. Mrs. 35	June 16, 1894
Hackney, D.G. 27	Reeves, Alice 17	December 28, 1890
Hackney, Ernest L. 23	Perry, Oleavia 19	January 27, 1917
Hackney, George 33	Jenkins, Ida 24	July 5, 1896
Hairston, E. 31	Brazton, Annie 26	November 12, 1900
Hall, B.F.	Lewis, Anna	(License Only) 1883
Hall, I.L. 28	Marshall, Frankie Mrs.	March 30, 1902
Hamble, Wm. 26	Cary, Anna 20	October 31, 1889
Hardy, A. 50	Brown, Alice 40	November 12, 1913
Harper, Joseph 33	Moss, Leona M. 21	September 7, 1909
Harris, Charles H. 22	Tolliver, Isabelle 21	September 29, 1881
Harris, Forriest 24	Bagby, Emma 19	December 31, 1907
Harris, George 22	Lewis, Gertrude B. 19	July 29, 1896
Harris, George 29	Turner, Mary 30	September 13, 1902
Harris, Hawkless 44	Bunt, Lou 34	February 19, 1885
Harris, Simon 30	Trent, Betty 35	(License Only) 1884
Harris, Simon 36	Claiborne, Cecelia 35	April 1, 1890
Harris, Simon 51	Harris, Celia 45	January 11, 1900
Harris, William 22	Gogan, Edith 19 (W)	October 6, 1900
Harshaw, George 23	Scroggins, Mollie 27	October 25, 1899
Hart, William 57	Taylor, Elizabeth 37	October 13, 1886
Harver, Lewis Wm. 29	Woods, Luceil 25	July 10, 1910
Harvey, John D. 36	Wright, Mary 36	June 17, 1919
Harvey, J. H. 41	Greerious, Jennie Meade	June 15, 1896
Harvey, Walter 27	Henderson, Pearl 19	(License Only) 1896
Hawkins, Henry Jr. 27	Vinson, Isabella 22	December 26, 1901

Before Buxton: The Muchakinock Years

Groom	Bride	Date
Helton, Fred 34	Murray, Mary 22	September 20, 1896
Henderson, Bert 27	Graves, Amanda 26	May 11, 1903
Henderson, Edward 25	Willias, Patty 20	October 26, 1898
Henderson, John 35	Dysart, Mabel 25	June 24, 1919
Henderson, Miner 28	Hoil, Ella	November 2, 1889
Hill, Ben 63	Dickison, Jane Mrs. 50	February 18, 1902
Hodge, Eugene B. 22	Gatewood, Bessie 20	December 15, 1896
Hodge, Robert W. 20	Findley, Nora A. 22	June 18, 1910
Holiday, Thomas 32	Johnson, Sarah 26	November 25, 1884
Holliday, James 25	Shepherd, Kizsie 22	(License Only) 1884
Holmes, Charles W. 19	Marshall, Iva 18	November 11, 1904
Hopkins, J.D. 31	Jones, Sadie E.	May 28, 1902
Howard, Robert 25	Broddus, Lizzie Mrs. 27	November 6, 1895
Hudgens, Charlie C. 23	Ferrall, Minnie 29	September 16, 1901
Hudgins, Ransome 46	Yates, Jane 40	May 21, 1888
Hudson, Nelson 35	Buchner, Ruby 19	December 3, 1917
Huggins, Ransome 63	Mitchell, Carrie 34	April 1900
Hughes, Williams 23	Robinson, Virginia 19	August 6, 1891
Hunter, Henry G. 33	Brown, Ella Holliday 28	January 7, 1902
Irvin, Samuel 27	Jackson, Elizabeth	August 18, 1890
Jackson, Andrew 27	Caldwell, Maggie 21	February 5, 1906
Jackson, Clarence 25	Johnson, Emma 18	November 1, 1900
Jackson, Clarence 36	Henderson, Bendy Mitchell 31	December 12, 1905
Jackson, George 22	Downey, Annie 20	November 9, 1893
Jackson, George 51	Gray, Alcy	July 9, 1901
Jackson, James 24	Bryant, Sallie Ann 19	December 14, 1901
Jackson, Robert 26	Howard, Bettie Call 24	October 23, 1886
Jackson, Robert 30	Banks, Susie 19	January 1, 1891
Jackson, Tom 35	Burkett, Lydia 22	January 17, 1914
James, Edward 35	Kelso, Kittie Powell 36	October 31, 1903
James, Spencer 31	Jackson, Mary Steward	January 14, 1888
James, Spencer 37	Cleysen, Belle 26	July 4, 1893
James, W.M. 30	Elfy, Rosetta 21	December 1, 1904
Jeffers, E.E. 34	Buckner, Lucy A. 33	March 5, 1901
Jefferson, Andrew J. 23	Taylor, Julia A.M. 16	December 28, 1893
Jefferson, Richard 23	Starcha, Eliza 26	February 16, 1897
Jenkins, Samuel 20	Brown, Ada 17	September 9, 1895
Jewet, Sargent 61	Allen, Mary 32	April 19, 1893

Jewett, Alfred 47	Brown, Lucy Wootsen 35	October 27, 1883
Johnson, A.J. 24	Winston, Lucy 28	March 15, 1888
Johnson, Charles A. 31	Walker, Mattie 31	February 20, 1893
Johnson, Edward 31	Trent, Belle 19	January 27, 1884
Johnson, Edward 39	Winston, Melissa Rogers 44	June 28, 1904
Johnson, Frank 26	Layafelt, May 27	December 10, 1901
Johnson, Galaway 24	Turner, Texas Mrs. 27	April 21, 1890
Johnson, Isaac P. 24	Dorsey, Nannie 23	November 29, 1882
Johnson, James 22	Logan, Anna 28	March 19, 1907
Johnson, John W. 23	Holliway, Anna 28	September 17, 1885
Johnson, J.T. 22	Hill, Ella M. 19	June 27, 1894
Johnson, Martin 50	Hennison, Lucinda Brooks 44	October 8, 1903
Johnson, Patrick 23	Anderson, Ada 22	September 29, 1885
Johnson, Patrick 32	Brown, Alice 23	April 19, 1896
Johnson, R.J. 27	Brockman, Mary F.	July 2, 1893
Johnson, R.J. 28	Hickman, Gladness 16	July 1, 1895
Johnson, R.J. 38	James, Annie Gibson 39	November 12, 1902
Johnson, Robert 22	None, Myar 22	October 20, 1884
Johnson, Robert 23	Allen, Mina 20	January 10, 1882
Johnson, Samson 27	Hughbanks, Adie 25	September 27, 1885
Johnson, Sherman 27	Allgood, Kittie 23 (W)	September 26, 1892
Johnson, W.D. 28	Nelson, Harriet R. 30	August 28, 1913
Johnson, Wilbur C. 27	Williams, Virginia 24	May 21, 1917
Johnson, William 22	Gaines, Annie 19	June 13, 1900
Jones, Albert 32	Washington, Sarah 28	March 24, 1885
Jones, Booker 35	Grimes, Maggie Harris 25	August 2, 1902
Jones, Charles 24	Poindexter, Emma 24	December 14, 1888
Jones, David Robert 48	Goins, Elizabeth 48	May 27, 1895
Jones, Edward F. 26	Wilson, Daisy E. 18	December 21, 1896
Jones, Floyd 32	Hogsett, Eliza 28	October 30, 1895
Jones, George 34	Evans, Jennie 23	October 16, 1919
Jones, Henry J. 22	Gillette, Fannie E. 19	(License Only) 1893
Jones, James 23	Carey, Gertrude 19	January 3, 1898
Jones, Jesse C. 26	Jackson, Edmonica 23	December 27, 1881
Jones, John 46	Snody, Mattie G. 44	September 9, 1912
Jones, Nathan 22	Carter, Ada 23 (W)	May 28, 1895
Jones, Richard T. 38	Martin, Elizabeth 43	December 7, 1893
Jones, Thomas 24	Yancy, Alice 22	August 19, 1895

Before Buxton: The Muchakinock Years

Jones, William 23	Jackson, Cornelia 19	July 3, 1900
Jones, William 22	Alexander, Maggie 19	October 26, 1898
Jones, Wilson 26	Frazier, Sarah 25	September 22, 1881
Jonsey, Robert H. 28	Anderson, Ada	May 25, 1892
Jordan, Amos 23	Dyer, Georgie 23	June 23, 1894
Kennie, Elmore	Lewis, Hager 23	January 27, 1881
King, Robert Jr. 27	Woods, Mary 20	November 28, 1889
King, William 25	Jackson, Etta 23	February 28, 1893
Knox, James 39	Garnett, Fannie 19	August 16, 1910
Lafayette, Jessie 24	Jant, Christina 18	February 17, 1900
Lafayette, Lewis W. 31	Clark, Lillie 19	February 25, 1903
Law, George 25	Edgar, Josephine 22	(License Only) 1886
Law, George 30	Dary, Carrie 18	October 17, 1895
Lawson, Ed 24	Boyous, Tina	November 23, 1898
Lee, Alonzo 33	Jones, Tillie 20	October 6, 1886
Lee, Daniel 26	Jones, Bettie 19	March 7, 1885
Lee, George E. 29	Martin, Ella Battles 24	December 13, 1899
Lee, John N. 28	Lightfoot, Ella 19	October 2, 1884
Lee, Henry L. 36	Taylor, Carrie 23	(License Only) 1890
Lee, Oscar G. 22	Kimbrough, Bernice 19	September 2, 1901
Leighton, Henry 26	Scott, Anna 23	April 14, 1885
Lenner, Joe 29	Watkins, Florence 19	August 24, 1895
Lewis, Christopher 23	Strange, Rosa 22	May 2, 1886
Lewis, Christopher 30	Jones, Martha 30	December 1, 1895
Lewis, Christopher 35	Henderson, Caroline 33	December 4, 1900
Lewis, Christopher 35	Boyers, Annie 46	December 5, 1900
Lewis, Geo. W. 24	Howard, Hattie 19	January 21, 1883
Lewis, J.B. 24	Goings, Jennie Brown 29	January 14, 1901
Lewis, J.H.	Drew, E.W. 24	March 25, 1883
Lewis, Vdell T. 21	Hart, Willa 20	October 17, 1906
Lewis, W.F. 31	Carson, Eliza	November 25, 1889
Lewis, W.W. 26	Harvey, Mary 25	October 19, 1891
Lincoln, Ed D. 31	Spraggs, Mary 27	November 13, 1894
Lipscomb, Robert 48	Moore, Annie 36	(License Only) 1901
Logan, Charles 28	White, Rosa 21	August 14, 1909
London, E.A. 26	Brown, Minnie B. 20	May 8, 1895
Loving, Adam 22	Chism, Belle 20	December 28, 1881
Lovings, Joe D. 24	Reesby, Paulina 20	November 24, 1885

LeeAnn Simmers Dickey

Lowry, James M. 35	Drew, Martha Ann 24	September 27, 1881
Lowry, Thomas 32	Anderson, Maggie 48	December 6, 1892
Lucas, Jeff 33	Miller, Lizzie Talley 38	May 3, 1896
Lucas, John B. 23	Craig, Dora 20	December 31, 1883
Madison, Frank 30	Carter, Alice 28	December 19, 1892
Maine, Charles 28	Wilson, Lottie M. Pope 28	March 23, 1888
Malory, J.O. 36	Williams, Lida 19	March 27, 1895
Marshall, Frank 26	Warren, Frankie 25	April 18, 1895
Marshall, George 22	Howard, Jennie 19	November 22, 1890
Marshall, George Jr. 22	Thomas, Julia 20	June 23, 1888
Marshall, Jesse 22	Earley, Viola 17	September 28, 1893
Marshall, William 22	Jones, Laura 18	June 12, 1884
Martin, Charles 30	Jefferson, Frances 27	(License Only) 1903
Masey, H.M. 24	Kinney, Alice 24	March 8, 1888
Massey, Horace 24	Cousin, Alice 21	February 2, 1889
Massey, Nicholas 27	Fry, Bertha 20	March 26, 1890
Mathens, Sam 23	Vivian, Rebecca 19	December 15, 1915
Mathews, Eugene 26	Webb, Ole 26	May 15, 1916
Mathews, John H. 28	Burgess, Alice 24	December 11, 1884
Mayo, Thos. Jr. 25	Starchey, Eliza	October 24, 1891
McCraven, Harry H. 20	Reeves, Elizabeth 24	August 22, 1900
McCutcheon, Henry 37	Bolden, Carrie 39	May 11, 1890
McDowell, J.H. 30	Anderson, Alice 23	July 3, 1890
McKinney, Norman 36	Bayers, Ethia 24	December 24, 1907
Mealy, Alphonzo 36	Dawsy, Ellen 22	August 28, 1884
Mease, C.H. 24	Tate, Cornelia 25	January 8, 1891
Mease, Jack 28	Osmond, Alice 27	January 24, 1889
Mease, Jackson 40	Toliver, Josephine 39	March 23, 1901
Mease, S.H. 25	Brown, Mary 19	February 20, 1889
Mickens, Ephram 22	Wheeler, Carrie 19	(License Only) 1907
Miles, Ed 25	Rhoades, Mary 19	June 28, 1894
Miller, Briscoe 29	Buckner, Carrie 19	September 23, 1890
Miller, C.G. 23	Jones, Maggie Alexander 20	November 12, 1900
Miller, Frank 33	Trent, Laura Mrs. 25	September 9, 1899
Miller, John 52	Sneed, Clara 31	September 18, 1904
Miller, Lewis 21	Jones, Florence 19	December 14, 1903
Miller, Samuel 24	Marshall, Mary A. 23	January 6, 1885
Miller, Samuel S. 27	Brown, Lucy 19	November 23, 1894

Before Buxton: The Muchakinock Years

Miller, W.M. 23	Hickman, Arie 19	December 26, 1896
Miller, Wallace 31	Wilson, Della 31	April 19, 1894
Mills, Edward T. 26	Smith, Ellen 22	August 31, 1881
Mills, J.E. 30	Mardis, Louada 30	June 18, 1913
Minnis, W.G. 28	Harris, Lizzie 27	December 25, 1884
Mitchell, Morris 37	Lewis, Hattie E. 30	November 29, 1894
Moore, John 26	Bolden, Gussie 20	November 4, 1912
Moore, Samuel 22	Bolden, Lula 16	January 24, 1885
Moore, William 47	Ward, Henrietta 43 (W)	June 4, 1888
Mooreman, H.C. 58	Scott, Ora M. Smith	October 21, 1914
Moorman, James 27	Overton, Betty 27	January 30, 1894
Moppin, James 23	Miller, Philenn 18	October 16, 1899
Morris, James H. 30	Douglass, Dollie A. 34	September 4, 1899
Morris, Walter B. 26	Brown, Estella 20	June 5, 1884
Mosby, Fred 23	Bolden, Rosa 20	August 9, 1894
Munroe, T.H. 27	Cary, Ada 19	October 3, 1888
Murray, J.L. 22	Leachman, Ollie	August 2, 1886
Nair, Guy S. 27 (W)	Toohey, Nellie C. 27	August 20, 1906
Neal, Albert 22	Washington, Mable 19	June 10, 1907
Neill, Richard T. 28	Ross, Susan 21	January 25, 1883
Nelson, Isaac 35	Murray, Bettie 30	November 15, 1891
Nelson, Rennie 23	Washington, Daisy 20	February 14, 1907
Nelson, Robert 29	Cotheran, Matilda 17	February 26, 1899
Nelson, Robert 38	Harvey, Blanche 26	June 17, 1916
Nichols, J.H. 22	Jackson, Etta 19	February 26, 1889
Nichols, J.H. 29	Scott, Maggie Mrs. 30	June 8, 1896
Nichols, J.H. 38	Brisco, Ethel 16	June 8, 1903
Niles, John B. 32	Harris, Sophia 21	May 21, 1883
Nolan, Lee 22	Williams, Alberta 19	April 15, 1899
Onsley, John E. 24	Mickle, Lee 23	April 1, 1903
Osburn, Cyrus 27	Woodson, Alice 24	August 18, 1885
Overton, J.W. 26	Freeman, Elizabeth Miller 25	November 24, 1887
Overton, Wesley 22	Lewis, Maggie 19	January 2, 1884
Overton, Wesley 35	Russell, Kate 38	January 8, 1897
Parker, Harry 22	Jones, Cornelia Jackson 22	September 15, 1903
Parker, Wiley 34	Clark, Mary 20	April 24, 1893
Parkey, Robt. L. 23	James, Oceola 22	November 3, 1920
Pasker, Thomas 39	Neal, Delia E. 22	(License Only) 1904

LeeAnn Simmers Dickey

Patterson, Charles 34	Shaddock, Ella 33 (W)	November 23, 1903
Payne, Richard 23	Taylor, Belle 19	December 27, 1902
Peaco, Samuel H. 46	Brown, Millie 42	June 16, 1915
Pergeson, Chas. 29	Darry, Martha 20	September 27, 1892
Perry, William K. 26	Brown, Melvina Hough 28	November 1, 1887
Petts, Austin 33	Griffin, Amanda E. 24	July 31, 1882
Plummer, James 40	Poer, Alice Buttram 42	April 23, 1921
Pointer, Arch 40	Everett, Alice Anna 25	September 23, 1901
Pollard, Andrew 32	Owens, Annie Mrs. 33	(License Only) 1880
Porterfield, James 26	Johnson, Willie 29	May 18, 1895
Porterfield, Richard 25	Carr, Marietta 23	October 23, 1889
Porterfield, Richard 35	Lee, Carrie 34	May 10, 1898
Porterfield, W.H. 28	Brown, Rosella 19	April 22, 1890
Price, Joseph 25	Wilson, Lena 21	December 31, 1890
Price, Richard 32	Washington, Margaret 20	June 9, 1881
Pritchett, William 22	Chaney, Mamie	October 21, 1899
Qualls, James 21	Williams, Cora 18	4 February 1892
Randall, George 35	Red, Hannah 24	December 25, 1880
Ray, Thomas 27	Bennett, Lelia M. 32	November 21, 1897
Reasby, Henry 21	Blakey, Mary 20	October 21, 1896
Reasby, J.N. 28	Bates, Bessie 19	June 13, 1900
Reasby, J.N. 30	Walker, Gertrude 21	July 26, 1902
Reasby, Lewis 27	Boyles, Lucy E. 21	July 9, 1896
Reasby, Noah 23	Brent, Annie 22	May 31, 1895
Reasby, Noah 28	Kelley, Mary Frances 18 (W)	April 8, 1903
Reasby, William 23	Sneade, Sarah James	May 23, 1888
Reed, Burkley 39	Strange, Annie E. Bates 30	August 23, 1889
Reeves, Alexander 34	Stepp, Fannie Brown 34	July 1, 1889
Reeves, James 42	Rowlen, Florence 30	September 18, 1890
Reeves, Nelson 47	Rushenbom, Laura J. 40	November 13, 1894
Reeves, Payton A. 22	Jones, Nellie 20	September 20, 1899
Reeves, W.H. 22	Logan, Ellen 18	April 23, 1896
Renix, James W. 30	Johnson, Alice M. 20	March 23, 1897
Rhodes, A.G. 45	Husted, Sarah 24	May 1898
Rhodes, Dennis 22	Brown, Nannie C. 19	April 22, 1890
Rhodes, W.C. 22	Dary, Lena 19	August 5, 1901
Richmond, W. Scott 28	Cosby, Bernice 25	October 5, 1910
Riggs, John W. 34	Logan, Elizabeth A. 35	February 27, 1894

Before Buxton: The Muchakinock Years

Roach, J.J. 28	Higbee, Myrtle 19	October 2, 1899
Robinson, Edward 47	Piece, Louisa 20	April 10, 1884
Robinson, Frank 23	Tanner, Rosa E. 19	November 2, 1891
Robinson, John S. 45	Scribner, Lillie 37	June 13, 1907
Robinson, Julius R. 28	Madison, Sina 29	September 9, 1902
Rollins, J.P. 43	Thompson, Lottie 37	(License Only) 1901
Rose, William 25	Terrill, Rose A. 21	October 23, 1903
Rowlett, John C. 37	Adams, Birdie A. 33	August 1, 1918
Rowley, George 24	Cooper, Goldie 25	April 27, 1904
Ruggles, Cole 26	Marvins, Gertrude 30	(License Only) 1908
Russell, Eugene Wm. 46	Lewis, Mabel 24	October 27, 1905
Russell, James E. Smith 56	Wilson, Fannie 56	December 25, 1916
Russell, Martin 22	Hickman, Etta 19	September 3, 1898
Schoolen, Gene 32	Derrick, Lucille 23	September 26, 1921
Scott, Benjamin 32	Coleman, Mary F. 17	February 4, 1892
Scott, Hillarus 47	Jones, Martha 40	August 6, 1885
Scott, J.H. 27	Johnson, Amanda 23	(License Only) 1901
Scott, Lee 24	Mickey, Florence 23	December 31, 1884
Scott, William 45	Brown, Maggie Carr 35	June 27, 1894
Shelton, Robert E. 26	Taylor, Minnie 19	August 12, 1897
Shepherd, James 26	Turner, Eliza Johnson 30	December 28, 1885
Sheppard, James 40	Reasby, Martha	January 2, 1900
Slaughter, King 27	Green, Caroline 23	December 26, 1883
Smith, Frank W. 48	Bell, Blanche M. 42	January 4, 1921
Smith, James 39	McDonald, Jennie 19	September 29, 1919
Smith, James 37	Edgar, Alice 30	October 5, 1889
Smith, James 24	Roberts, Sarah N. 21	October 25, 1899
Smith, James 51	Jefferson, Easter 49	June 13, 1900
Smith, John 33	Wilson, Sally 17	April 20, 1900
Smith, Henry 43	Buckner, Julia Waterford 32	November 14, 1883
Smith, Livine 29	Taylor, Edna 22	August 27, 1903
Smith, Lorenzo 19	Fields, Ada 20	April 24, 1906
Smith, Oscar B. 25	Reeves, Mollie 18	December 25, 1888
Smith, Thomas H. 27	Sprague, Ida 19	December 25, 1893
Smith, W.H. 22	Brown, Emma 20	February 14, 1901
Smith, William 34	Williams, Lattie 34	October 23, 1915
Sorrell, Joseph 26	Bates, Antonia 18	(License Only) 1890
Sorrell, Phil 26	Miller, Eva 19	March 11, 1895

LeeAnn Simmers Dickey

Soto, Frank 35 (Mex)	Jerrel, Lulu 45 (B)	May 16, 1918
Southall, Alex 27	Harris, Amay	(License Only) 1886
Southall, Charles G. 28	Young, Julia E. 26	August 11, 1891
Southall, Henry 29	Southall, Anne Harris 45	March 21, 1901
Spears, John W. 30	Hawkins, Anna E. 20	October 25, 1888
Staples, J.A. 27	Curry, Sallie 19	November 20, 1893
Strange, Patrick 23	Bates, Anne E. 24	July 25, 1883
Strange, P.T. 30	Quarles, Rhoda 31	August 15, 1891
Stewart, Maborn 30	Adams, Mollie 33	September 9, 1915
Stewart, Thos. 28	Bryant, Sophia	June 24, 1917
Stovall, James L. 28	Harvy, Lucy 17	January 19, 1901
Stribling, Cyrus 24	Quarles, Roda 22	March 10, 1881
Strong, Henry 60	Lewis, Matilda 66	September 23, 1893
Strouther, Lud 23	Willis, Georganie 23	October 10, 1894
Strowder, Alfred 51	Carter, Frances 22	January 28, 1886
Tayler, T.F. 31	Jones, Alice 23	October 9, 1899
Taylor, Barclay C. 34	Porterfield, Clara 22	February 24, 1900
Taylor, Clark 29	Johnson, Nora 29	June 2, 1921
Taylor, Ernest 22	Douglas, Nannie 19	November 23, 1897
Taylor, Ernest 24	Dickerson, Tona M. 16	September 4, 1912
Taylor, George E. 36	Buckner, Cora E. 21	August 25, 1894
Taylor, George W. 36	Barnes, Hattie 32	(License Only) 1885
Taylor, Henry 46	Lewis, Lizzie 32	April 12, 1885
Taylor, Henry 65	Burks, Minnie 48	October 31, 1906
Taylor, Zacharia 27	Thompson, Bessie 17	June 29, 1890
Thomas, Dabney 33	Taylor, Hattie 17	February 26, 1888
Thomas, Jeff 37	Hindricka, Mattie 35 (W)	April 1, 1901
Thomas, John 35	Stevenson, Elizabeth	December 7, 1903
Thomas, N.G. 32	Anderson, Nellie 30	December 11, 1894
Thomas, William 24	Brown, Emma 21	January 3, 1900
Thompson, Jewell 23	Hughes, Etta Mae	April 11, 1917
Thompson, Henry 37	Morris, Belle 40	May 29, 1898
Thornton, W.H. 27	Davis, Alice 28	November 1, 1882
Tiffin, F.D. 29	Monteen, Hattie B. 22	September 27, 1902
Tiffin, James 21	Shaw, Mary 20	October 31, 1886
Tinson, Alfred H. 38	Hurt, Lovenia 19	February 20, 1892
Todd, Charles 41	Simpson, Emma Austin 42	April 16, 1904
Toney, James 28	Jasper, Mary 26	April 11, 1901

Before Buxton: The Muchakinock Years

Toney, William M. 24	Straughter, Malinda 29	December 25, 1894
Topson, C.F. 39	Beashers, Lizzie 28	November 25, 1897
Toliver, Thomas 32	Rhodes, Josephine 36	January 4, 1898
Truehart, Jerry 28	Shelton, Hannah 26	December 8, 1885
Truehart, William 26	Harris, Josie 24	May 9, 1899
Trusty, William 38	Wilson, Sarah 29	October 13, 1892
Turner, Fleming 22	Desper, Texie 19	August 29, 1888
Turner, Madison 47	Veny, Phebe Kinney 39	November 26, 1891
Turner, Theodore 32	Jones, Jessie E. 27	December 2, 1909
Turner, Thomas 23	Steward, Elnora	May 2, 1888
Turner, Willis 22	Jones, Georgia 20	July 23, 1889
Underwood, Samuel D. 31	Hawkins, Leta 25	August 21, 1902
Vanderden, Franklin 42	Jenkins, Hester Lions 46	January 1, 1892
Vandergriff, Dean 33	Walker, Maime 19	October 29, 1898
Waddy, Andrew 28	Miller, Sarah 17	December 27, 1893
Walker, C.M. 43	Henderson, Caroline 33	December 4, 1900
Walker, Dyer Jr. 23	Lewis, Ella 25	July 28, 1884
Walker, F.T. 22	Burgess, Nellie 19	November 8, 1881
Walker, G.W. 25	Smith, Lucy 35	March 24, 1890
Walker, George W. 35	Mago, Rena 34	October 25, 1885
Walker, Harry 33	Kinner, Victoria 22	November 29, 1917
Walker, Henry 50	Johnson, Amanda 25	May 12, 1907
Walker, Henry 42	Malone, Bynky 50	December 9, 1901
Walker, John 31	Pritchet, Mattie 25	(License Only) 1886
Walker, John M. 39	Lawson, Sarah 21	December 26, 1893
Walker, Nelson 26	Blankford, Mary 21	October 7, 1886
Walker, Nelson 29	Williams, Millie	December 29, 1890
Walker, R.J. 30	Byers, Emma 30	June 13, 1899
Walker, Robert 27	Rhodes, Mary 21	December 28, 1898
Wallace, John 23	Smith, Emma 19	August 27, 1885
Ward, Harrison 33	Ringo, Stella 34	April 15, 1921
Warren, Robert 85	Atwater, Charity 83	June 4, 1897
Washburn, Joseph 33	Collins, Lizzie B. 29	July 12, 1888
Washington, Edward 24	Lewis, Henrieta 20	July 8, 1886
Washington, Geo. 48	Williams, Hannah Mrs. 50	February 18, 1918
Washington, James H. 25	Graves, Betty E. 19	October 26, 1882
Washington, John F. 25	White, Blanch V. 21	March 6, 1901
Washington, William F. 23	Perkins, Willa 19	May 5, 1902

LeeAnn Simmers Dickey

Watson, Jacob 28	Mines, Julia 24	December 26, 1888
Watson, Robert 27	Smith, Ella 23	April 14, 1900
Welch, Julius 20	Williams, Annie 19	August 1898
Wesley, James 26	McKinney, Sarah 22	January 25, 1888
Western, George 55	Haggan, Lou Cooper 50	March 25, 1898
Wheeler, Clyde B. 22	Martin, Eugena May 19	June 15, 1914
White, A.W. 47 (W)	Freeman, Sarah 39	December 9, 1899
White, George 53	Mattison, Betty Mrs. 57	December 9, 1895
White, James 23	Kelley, Clara Bell 18	October 23, 1905
White, Joseph 25	Williams, Henriette 23	October 25, 1892
White, Sam 24	Jackson, Laura F. 30	December 31, 1909
Wiles, Lewis A. 23	Bess, Judith E. 28	November 21, 1883
Wiles, L.A. 38	Frazier, Dora 27	December 29, 1897
Wilson, Arthur 22	Douglas, Emma 19	September 4, 1900
Willhoit, Walter 24	Allgood, Emma Bell 18	August 15, 1906
Williams, Andrew 24	Buckner, Babe 35	June 9, 1921
Williams, Ed 30	Nelson, Ida 19	February 1, 1897
Williams, George 31	Grandison, Lizzie 38	July 15, 1897
Williams, Henry 37	Robison, Rosa 21	April 16, 1896
Williams, John 35	White, Emma 27	January 30, 1894
Williams, John E. 43	Lewis, Annie	November 28, 1896
Williams, John S. 24	Earkine, Mary J. 32	November 28, 1880
Williams, John W. 52	Smith, Sarah 47	October 20, 1892
Williams, John W. 48	Henton, Eliza H. 51	February 21, 1910
Williams, Oscar 24	Richmond, Matilda 22	May 25, 1893
Williams, Peter 64	Smith, Hannah 46	September 13, 1900
Williams, T.J. 39	Moorman, Bettie 36	June 23, 1903
Williams, Walter 24	Ross, Catherine 22	September 15, 1885
Williams, William 29	Vinson, Bertha 21	October 28, 1903
Willis, Edward 41	Taylor, Emma	(License Only) 1894
Willis, George 28	Gibbons, Lulu 21	April 17, 1903
Willis, George E. 22	Wright, Georgia E. 19	November 6, 1895
Wilson, Adolph W. 22	Pugh, Effie 19	April 12, 1906
Wilson, Arthur 22	Douglas, Emma 19	September 4, 1900
Wilson, Joseph 24	Lucas, Gertrude 19	(License Only) 1885
Wilson, J.W. 53	Findley, Fannie	October 29, 1894
Wilson, Samuel 39	Brock, Maggie 24	December 14, 1887
Wilson, Wesley 32	Pondexter, Dory 25	October 26, 1890

Before Buxton: The Muchakinock Years

Wing, Joseph 39	Johnson, Myra 26	November 3, 1883
Wolfskill, Zall 24	Shields, Lizzie L. 22	March 18, 1907
Wood, W.H. 22	Jones, Alice 20	March 28, 1889
Wood, W.M. 22	Moppins, Josie 16	February 12, 1887
Wood, Wesley 23	Gillett, Eliza	April 29, 1891
Woodford, Isaac 30	Striblin, Anna 25	April 3, 1888
Woodson, Berman 24	Brent, Anna 28	April 11, 1903
Wootson, Thomas C. 26	Jefferson, Ella 21	March 11, 1883
Wormley, William 24	Mays, Amanda 19	November 3, 1881
Wright, Alfred L. 29	Coleman, Minnie B. 19	December 23, 1908
Wright, Glenn 28	Thomas, Josephine Himes 20	October 5, 1887
Wright, Hiram 24	Desper, Jennie 21	April 22, 1886
Wright, John 35	Douglas, Claudia L. 23	March 25, 1909
Wright, Robert 22	Taylor, Emma McLee 19	March 15, 1906
Yancy, G.D. 28	Husted, Myrtle 19 (W)	May 1899
Young, Gus 25	Taylor, Edna 18	March 7, 1900
Young, John M. 35	Brown, Anna 31	July 9, 1907

Buxton, Iowa, depot and train yards. Date not known. (Courtesy of Robert Thompson)

LeeAnn Simmers Dickey

Muchakinock Cemetery Records

Muchakinock Cemetery is an abandoned pioneer cemetery located in East Des Moines Township, Mahaska County, Iowa in Section 13. It is located on a farm with foot access only, about one mile south of where the company store was located. It is 3.2 acres and is located on land which was first owned by H. A. Armstrong.

Information is given in the following order: Name; race if available; death date; age; cause of death if available; source of information. An asterisk after the name indicates that there is a stone marking this grave in the cemetery.

Adams, Hezekiah. Black. September 4, 1889. 29 years. Typhoid Fever. McCurdy Funeral Home.

Allen, Cora. December 1, 1886. 5 years. Diphtheria. Mahaska Co. Death Record.

Anderson, Anthony. August 25, 1885. 8 months. Mahaska Co. Death Record.

Anderson, Mrs. C.M. (Fina). January 2, 1885. 22 years. Typhoid Fever. Mahaska Co. Death Record.

Archer, Isabella. Black. July 29, 1895. 10 months 18 days. Cholera Infantum. Hank Archer.

Archer, Mary Jane. April 27, 1898. 39 years. Pneumonia. John Chapman.

Archer, William H. May 21, 1897. 54 years 5 months. Rheumatism. C.R. Foster.

Archer, Lizzie A. October 25, 1898. 19 months. Lung Fever. Shane Arthur.

Ayers, Charles. Black. February 4, 1885. 35 years. Inflammation. McCurdy Funeral Home.

Barber, Mrs. Flora. Black. October 14, 1883. 65 years. Dropsy. McCurdy Funeral Home.

Baxter, William. December 19, 1900. 44 years 6 months. C.R. Foster.

Bingham, Mary Lathen. September 16, 1900. 14 years 4 months 28 days. Cholera Infantum. Monroe County Death Record.

Blakey, Anna. Black. September 10, 1884. 7 years. Consumption. McCurdy Funeral Home.

Blakey, Daughter of Simon. Black. June 26, 1886. 7 years. Scofula. McCurdy Funeral Home.

Blakey, Lucindy. July 29, 1890. 30 years 6 months. Mahaska Co. Death Record.

Blakey, Mary. Black. April 6, 1886. 5 years. McCurdy Funeral Home.

Blakey, Sarah. Black. September 6, 1885. 16 years. Instantaneous. McCurdy Funeral Home.

Before Buxton: The Muchakinock Years

Bolden, John. Black. January 11, 1889. 53 years. Excelisor Mine. McCurdy Funeral Home.

Bolden, John. August 3, 1889. 1 year 2 months. Lung Fever. McCurdy Funeral Home.

Bolden, John. Black. March 15, 1888. 54 years 4 months 1 day. Heart/ Dropsy. McCurdy Funeral Home.

Booker, George. Black. December 15, 1883. 85 years. Gravel. McCurdy Funeral Home.

Boyers, Samuel. January 20, 1898. Mahaska Co. Death Record.

Brashton, William. December 9, 1900. 47 years 5 months. Pneumonia. Monroe County Death Record.

Brown, Clarence. Black. March 29, 1895. 2 weeks. C. Brown.

Brown, Daughter of C. Black. September 6, 1884. 4 months. McCurdy Funeral Home.

Brown, Inf. Daughter of C. Black. September 22, 1894. 6 months. C. Brown/ McCurdy Funeral.

Brown, Louise. Black. November 17, 1887. 1 year 1 month 7 days. Pneumonia. McCurdy Funeral Home.

Brown, Meshue. September 28, 1893. 7 months 3 days. Mahaska Co. Death Record.

Brown, Okalomie. March 13, 1893. 1 year 1 month 14 days. Mahaska Co. Death Record.

Brown, R. J. Black. July 26, 1896. 41 years. Fever. McCurdy Funeral Home.

Brown, Son of R. J. Black. April 5, 1888. 5 years. Gun Accident. McCurdy Funeral Home.

Bryant, Heney Retta. Black. November 21, 1899. 13 years 3 months. Diphtheria. W.A.Wells Co.

Bryant, Henrietta. November 12, 1900. 12 years 6 months 12 days. McCurdy Funeral Home.

Burke, Mrs. Georgena. June 14, 1897. 72 years 8 months. Paralysis. W.A. Wells Co.

Burkes, John. Black. March 9, 1891. 3 years 6 months 9 days. Spinal. McCurdy Funeral Home.

Burkett, Lottie. February 11, 1897. 74 years. Mahaska Co. Death Record.

Butler, Howard. Black. November 5, 1885. 28 years. Fever. McCurdy Funeral Home.

Callins, Isaac. November 6, 1903. 87 years. Dropsy. Relatives.

Canaday, Creed. * Black. March 15, 1889. 1 month 6 days. (Stone has March 18, 1889). McCurdy Funeral Home.

Canaday, Emiline A. Black. September 30, 1892. 62 years. Bowels. McCurdy Funeral Home.

Carey, H. Lucial. September 23, 1900. 22 years 5 months 7 days. C.R. Foster & W. Carey.

Carey, Wilson. November 29, 1897. 75 years. Old Age. Wilson Carey.

Carlson, Otto Sanford. March 16, 1901. 6 years 3 months. Diphtheria. Monroe County Death Record.

Carr, Fricker. Black. January 14, 1884. 27 years. Typhoid Fever. McCurdy Funeral Home.

Carr, Tucker. * February 15, 1884. 22 years 10 months 9 days. Son of H. & G. Carr.

Carter, Unnamed. May 10, 1894. 5 years. Dropsy. W.A. Wells Co.

Carter, Unnamed. October 19, 1896. 25 years. Mahaska Co. Death Record.

Carter, Anna. Black. April 12, 1893. 35 years. Cheeseman Funeral Home.

Carter, Effie. July 14, 1889. 1 year 10 months. Cholera Infantum. McCurdy Funeral Home.

Carter, Jack. Black. July 2, 1884. 26 years. Fever. McCurdy Funeral Home.

Caul, George S. Black. January 11, 1887. 28 years. Consumption. McCurdy Funeral Home.

Cary, Tessie Deatris. November 1898. 5 months. Mahaska Co. Death Record.

Chambers, Jeanetta. June 18, 1899. 4 months. Spasms. W.A. Wells Co.

Chapman, Clarence E.* November 25, 1892. 22 years 15 days. Typhoid Fever. McCurdy Funeral Home.

Chapman, James Bell.* March 25, 1895. 32 years 1 month 22 days. Bowels. W.A. Wells Co.

Coghill, Ethel. January 12, 1897. 11 months 23 days. Mahaska Co. Death Record.

Coleman, Arthur E.* May 19, 1883. 34 years 5 months 3 days. Son of T.A. & M.J. Coleman.

Coles, Joe. October 1, 1893. 24 years. Malaria Fever. McCurdy Funeral Home.

Collins, Mrs. Armison (Maria). March 23, 1903. 72 years. Dropsy. Tabernacle Lodge - Buxton, Iowa.

Collins, Isaac. November 6, 1903. 71 years. Mahaska Co. Death Record.

Cosby, Temper. Black. January 7, 1887. 38 years. Accident- Frozen. McCurdy Funeral Home.

Cowins, Polly. Black. June 23, 1887. 84 years. Typhoid Fever. McCurdy Funeral Home.

Crosby, Titus. Black. February 15, 1889. 26 years. Mine Accident. McCurdy Funeral Home.

Curry, Infant of Wm. November 18, 1896. Mahaska Co. Death Record.

Before Buxton: The Muchakinock Years

Dade, Joseph. Black. October 16, 1884. Paralysis. McCurdy Funeral Home.

Daid, Mrs. Anna. Black. September 30, 1884. 49 years. Malaria Fever. McCurdy Funeral Home.

Dixon, Ardaville F. Black. May 18, 1895. 7 years 10 months 19 days. Fever. Adam Dixon.

Dixon, James E. Black. March 24, 1896. 1 year 3 months 11 days. Fever. Adam Dixon.

Dorsey, William. Black. March 27, 1885. 38 years. Killed in Mine. McCurdy Funeral Home.

Douglas, Pearlieo.* October 31, 1889. Mahaska Co. Death Record.

Douglass, Lusella. (also listed as **Duglass, Lusella**) May 22, 1899. 1 day. Mahaska Co. Death Record.

Douglass, Mrs. Black. September 15, 1893. Dropsy. McCurdy Funeral Home.

Downey, Emmet. Black. October 23, 1886. 9 years. Diphtheria. McCurdy Funeral Home.

Drew, Frank M. Black. April 19, 1893. 26 years 6 months 2 days. Internal Hemorrhage. McCurdy Funeral Home.

Drew, Fredrick Douglas. May 4, 1900. 21 years 11 months 16 days. Lowery and Monroe.

Drew, George Thomas. Black. October 7, 1892. 1 month 16 days. Indigestion. McCurdy Funeral Home.

Drew, Helena. November 10, 1897. 9 years. Croup. Robert Drew.

Drew, John R. April 4, 1895. 43 years 5 months 8 days. Consumption. Lowery & Monroe.

Drew, Viola. September 27, 1899. 2 years 9 months. Croup. J.W. Riggs.

Drew, Willie. November 12, 1897. Croup. Father.

Early, Maggie. May 9, 1897. 22 years 9 days. Mahaska Co. Death Record.

Fennell, John. (also listed as **Ferrell, John.**) Black. February 3, 1884. 28 years. Mine Accident. McCurdy Funeral Home.

Fielding, Adam. August 3, 1900. 56 years 3 months. Wilson Carey Lodge.

Fielding, Gertrude. July 5, 1902. 53 years 6 months. Heart Disease. Monroe County Death Record.

Fielding, Unknown. * March 30, 1882. No age given.

Foster, James Lawson.* November 25, 1898. 41 years 4 months 11 days. Heart. C.R. Foster.

Fox Chief Cooper. Indian. November 27, 1887. 24 years. Alcohol- Found Dead. McCurdy Funeral Home.

Franklin, Sam. December 13, 1900. 58 years. Brain. C.R. Foster.

LeeAnn Simmers Dickey

Frazier, G. W. May 1, 1895. No age given.

Gaines, Maggie. Black. March 19, 1888. 24 years. Consumption. Mahaska Co. Death Record.

Garland, Ed. (Son of Julia). June 15, 1897. No age given.

Gibbins, Jessie E. October 14, 1902. 16 years 2 months 25 days. Mrs. Tom Gibbins.

Gillett, C.A. June 1, 1893. 26 years. Consumption. McCurdy Funeral Home.

Gillett, Julia.* Black. October 3, 1892. 22 years 8 months 22 days. Consumption. McCurdy Funeral Home.

Gillette, Alonzo. September 11, 1892. 10 months 21 days. Inflammation of Bowels. McCurdy Funeral Home.

Glaughlin, Maggie. May 9, 1897. 22 years. Consumption. C.R. Foster.

Gordon, Mrs. Ella. Black. December 26, 1884. 17 years. Typhoid Fever. McCurdy Funeral Home.

Green, Malinda. January 25, 1899. 70 years. Lung Trouble. Reuben Gaines.

Gregg, Mrs. Nannie. Black. August 8, 1894. 19 years. Consumption. F. Lofland Co.

Grene, Benny W. January 25, 1902. 23 years. Lung Fever. Monroe County Death Record.

Guy, Pearlie. November 10, 1900. 9 years. Consumption. Stephen Guy.

Hackney, Luetta. Black. April 5, 1894. 2 years 2 months 4 days. Cheeseman Funeral Home.

Hailey, William. February 17, 1899. 33 years. Dropsy. Wilson Carey.

Harris, Mrs. Harkless. Black. April 21, 1884. 56 years. Erysipelas. McCurdy Funeral Home.

Harris, Infant of Lucy. August 22, 1890. 4 months. Cholera Infantum. McCurdy Funeral Home.

Harris, Lucy E. December 23, 1899. 25 years 6 months 20 days. Consumption. G.D. Harris.

Harvey, Amanda.* Black. September 29, 1889. 56 years 9 months. Inflammation of Bowels. McCurdy Funeral Home.

Harvey, Amanda. Black. August 25, 1884. 3 years. Cholera Infantum. McCurdy Funeral Home.

Harvey, Jessie. Black. September 24, 1888. 7 months. Cholera Infantum. McCurdy Funeral Home.

Harvey, Louis.* Black. March 16, 1887. 71 years 5 months 7 days. Old Age. Mahaska Co. Death Record.

Harvey, Mrs. Lucy. Black. April 12, 1891. 30 years. Inflammation of Bowels. McCurdy Funeral Home.

Before Buxton: The Muchakinock Years

Hawkins, Daughter of John. Black. November 18, 1885. 10 months. Cholera Infantum. McCurdy Funeral Home.

Hawkins, Elizabeth. November 6, 1892. Mahaska Co. Death Record.

Hawkins, George Thomas. Black. June 10, 1896. 18 years 2 months 9 days. Consumption. Charles Neese.

Hawkins, Joseph. October 5, 1890. 55 years 10 months 18 days. Dysentery/ Flux. McCurdy Funeral Home.

Hawkins, Child of John. Black. September 20, 1883. Cholera Infantum. McCurdy Funeral Home.

Hawkins, Robert. January 1, 1881. 6 years 5 months 15 days. Mahaska Co. Death Record.

Henderson, Mrs. John. Black. October 8, 1894. 40 years. Consumption. W.A. Wells Co.

Henderson, Joseph. August 10, 1902. 18 years 6 months. Consumption. Mother.

Hogan, Cora. Black. August 11, 1884. 3 years. McCurdy Funeral Home.

Hughes, Mason. March 24, 1902. 42 years. Dropsy. J.H. Lewis.

Hughes, William H. Black. August 12, 1896. 55 years. C.R. Foster.

Hunt, Infant twin of A.B. June 10, 1899. 10 days. Convulsions. W.A. Wells Co.

Huston, Ada Elizabeth. May 19, 1899. Mahaska Co. Death Record.

Jackson, Edward. April 2, 1900. 3 years 10 days. Lung Fever. George Jackson

Jackson, Linford Carl. February 8, 1900. 5 months 11 days. W.A. Wells Co.

Jefferson, Jennie. Black. September 4, 1883. 20 years. Consumption. McCurdy Funeral Home.

Jefferson, Mrs. Polly. Black. August 29, 1890. 63 years. Paralysis. McCurdy Funeral Home.

Jett, Earnest. Black. June 16, 1884. 10 years. Fever. McCurdy Funeral Home.

Jewett, Mrs. Albert (Lucy). February 13, 1890. 49 years 1 month 21 days. Croup / Colic. McCurdy Funeral Home.

Johnson, Chanie. Black. March 27, 1894. 76 years. Old Age. Sampson Johnson.

Johnson, Daughter of Mrs. Black. September 29, 1884. 6 months. Cholera Infantum. Sampson Johnson.

Johnson, Dora. December 26, 1902. 18 years. Consumption. E.D. Johnson.

Johnson, Lizzie. May 24, 1887. 17 years 11 months 19 days. Consumption. E.D. Johnson.

Johnson, Phineas. Black. February 4, 1884. 3½ years. Brain Fever. McCurdy Funeral Home.

Johnson, Terry. Black. November 5, 1889. Lung Fever. Mahaska Co. Death Record.

LeeAnn Simmers Dickey

Jones, Alice. Black. June 20, 1900. 45 years 7 months 1 day. Paralysis/ Rheumatism. Monroe County Death Record.
Jones, Infant of Floyd (Robert). May 8, 1902. 8 months. Pneumonia. Father.
Jones, Infant of W. J. Black. December 12, 1884. 7 days. McCurdy Funeral Home.
Jones, Rameo. December 6, 1903. 26 years 3 months 3 days. Lung Trouble. W.J. Jones.
Jones, Robert. May 27, 1901. 53 years. Pneumonia. W.A. Wells Co.
Jones, Mrs. Robert (Lucy Ellen). Black. April 6, 1894. 48 years. Paralysis. Husband- W.A. Wells Co.
Jones, Sallie Ann. Black. May 4, 1896. 47 years 11 months 17 days. Cheeseman Funeral Home.
Jones, Son of William. December 11, 1883. 7 years. Burned. McCurdy Funeral Home.
Jones, W. P. October 15, 1901. 36 years. Pneumonia. C.R. Foster.
Karr, H. M. November 16, 1892. 3 years 9 months. Fever. McCurdy Funeral Home.
Kennedy, Julia. Black. April 15, 1884. 12 years. Typhoid Pneumonia. McCurdy Funeral Home.
Kinney, Ann. Black. February 24, 1888. 66 years. Dropsy. McCurdy Funeral Home.
Kinney, Clarence. January 18, 1897. 11 months 6 days. Lung. L.W. Kinney.
Kinney, Isaac. Black. July 23, 1889. 40 years. Dysentery. McCurdy Funeral Home.
Lash, Elmer. February 12, 1897. 42 years. Prog. Neuritis. Tom Carlin.
Lawson, Mrs. Kate. February 22, 1900. 34 years. Dropsy. J.W. Lawson.
Lewis, Daughter of Andy. Black. October 15, 1884. 3 months. Cholera Infantum. McCurdy Funeral Home.
Lewis, Infant of J. L. October 7, 1895. 10 days. Mrs. Mones.
Lewis, John W. November 14, 1883. 21 years. Consumption. Mahaska Co. Death Record.
Logan, Mrs. Hattie. Black. February 12, 1895. 25 years. Consumption. John S. & Wells Co.
London, William E.* Black. December 26, 1897. 3 months 20 days. Son of W.H. & M.B. London.
Long, Infant. October 6, 1899. 0 years. W.A. Wells Co.
Long, Infant of Ann. June 28, 1893. 1 day. Mahaska Co. Death Record.
Lukes, David. August 1898. 50 years. Mahaska Co. Death Record.
Madison, Frank. July 20, 1899.
Martin, Edmond/ Edward. Black. July 6, 1893. 65 years. Cheeseman Funeral Home.
Martin, Ella. December 6, 1901. 9 months 4 days. Dropsy. Bettie Martin.
Matthews, Mrs. Tilley. June 21, 1897. 36 years. Tumor. S. Matthews.

Before Buxton: The Muchakinock Years

Mays, Lottie. Black. April 11, 1890. 3 months. Lung Fever. McCurdy Funeral Home.
Mays, W. Spencer. March 2, 1901. 51 years. Consumption. Wilson Carey (Also listed as Stomach & Liver/Monroe County Death Record).
McDowell, Bessie. Black. August 2, 1887. 1 year 6 months. Diphtheria. McCurdy Funeral Home.
McDowell, Gorganna. Black. March 8, 1893. 35 years 1 month 11 days. Miscarriage. McCurdy Funeral Home.
Miles, Baxter. December 1, 1899. 40 years. Chilled Spice. Coroner.
Miller, Elizabeth Isabella. Black. October 12, 1893 (1898?). 34 years 5 months 3 days. Wife of John Miller.
Mills, Infant of Edward. Black. February 5, 1892. McCurdy Funeral Home.
Miner, George E. Black. January 18, 1884. 29 years. Scrofula. McCurdy Funeral Home.
Mines, Bettie R. September 3, 1888.
Mines, Mrs. Rhetta E. Black. August 30, 1888. 28 years. Fever. McCurdy Funeral Home.
Moore, Ashby. January 15, 1893. 9 years. Mahaska Co. Death record.
Morman, Harry. Black. September 4, 1902. 3 months 5 days. Mahaska Co. Death Record.
Morman, Sellis. July 6, 1899. 1 year 3 months 4 days. Mahaska Co. Death Record.
Noe, Infant of B. September 25, 1896. W.E. Gladwin.
Nolan, Obry. February 25, 1901. 6 months 20 days. Lung Fever. Monroe County Death Record.
Norman, Son of John. August 23, 1898. 1 year 6 months. W.A. Wells Co.
Nowlan, Infant. February 25, 1901. 6 months. Lung Fever. W.A. Wells Co.
Osborn, Cyrus. Black. August 26, 1887. 29 years 13 days. Crushed in Mine. McCurdy Funeral Home.
Padgett, Chas. August 1895. No age given.
Padgett, Margaret. June 28, 1900. 59 years. Dropsy. W.A. Wells Co.
Padgett, William. July 5, 1901. 78 years. Mine Accident. Wilson Carey.
Peoco, Richemmaline. September 8, 1894. 56 years 9 months 5 days. Dropsy. N.B. McDowell.
Porterfield, S. Black. May 21, 1896. 6 years 3 months. Gunshot. Charles Foster.
Rawlings, Edward. March 29, 1891. 61 years 1 month. Mahaska Co. Death Record.
Reasby, Mrs. Bessie. Black. May 21, 1896. 17 years. Bone. Noah Reasby.
Reasby, Infant of Henry. June 9, 1897. 3 months.

Reasby, James G.* Black. August 4, 1882. Son of L. & M. Reasby

Reasby, Louis. Black. October 17, 1886. 55 years. Scrofula. McCurdy Funeral Home.

Reasby, Martha J.* Black. June 22, 1880. Daughter of L. & M. Reasby.

Reed, Julia W. June 20, 1898. 71 years 1 month 18 days. Kidney. W.A. Wells Co.

Reeves, Mrs. Bertha. Black. February 23, 1895. 35 years. Consumption. Ruth #312

Reeves, Ethel. Black. April 15, 1894. 8 months. Pneumonia. Gladwin.

Reeves, Henrietta. Black. April 5, 1887. 7 years. Rheumatism. McCurdy Funeral Home.

Reeves, James. Black. January 24, 1888. 11 years 23 days. Typhoid Fever. McCurdy Funeral Home.

Reeves, Pearl C. August 13, 1898. 1 year 6 months 6 days. Teething. W.A. Wells Co.

Reeves, Son of Peter. November 20, 1892. 0 day. Stillborn. McCurdy Funeral Home.

Rhoades, Addines. September 10, 1887. 3 years. Heart. McCurdy Funeral Home.

Rhoades, Baby. August 18, 1898. 21 days. W.A. Wells Co.

Rhoades, Baby. August 19, 1898. Cooper Co.

Rhoades, Infant of Ed. November 20, 1892. 1 month 14 days. Inability. McCurdy Funeral Home.

Rhoades, Maggie. Black. July 19, 1894. 2 ¼ years. Cholera Infantum. Sam Rhoades.

Rhoades, Unnamed. April 7, 1901. W.A. Wells Co.

Rhoades, W.A. January 31, 1887. 45 years. Pneumonia. McCurdy Funeral Home.

Rhodes, Elfie. December 1897. 15 years.

Rhodes, Jane. February 6, 1895. No age given.

Rhodes, Lucy. Black. July 15, 1884. 3 months. Brain Fever. McCurdy Funeral Home.

Rhodes, William Edward. April 7, 1901. 19 years. Lung Trouble. Monroe County Death Record.

Ridgway, Robert Lee. July 28, 1899. 20 years 10 months. Brain Fever. Monroe County Death Record.

Roberts, Cora. November 21, 1884. 9 years. Fever. McCurdy Funeral Home.

Roberts, Lucille. October 6, 1900. 5 years 5 months 13 days. Typhoid Fever. Monroe County- Leonard Roberts.

Robinson, Mrs. Ned. August 12, 1895. No age given.

Robinson, Sadie.* July 10, 1880. 3 months 24 days. Daughter of L. & M. Robinson.

Before Buxton: The Muchakinock Years

Ross, Posey. September 10, 1885. 1 ½ years. General Debility. McCurdy Funeral Home.
Scott, Emma. March 3, 1894. 1 ½ years. Brain. F.A. Coleman.
Scott, Mylic. Black. August 22, 1893. 9 months. Cholera Infantum. McCurdy Funeral Home.
Seams, Unnamed Male. June 8, 1897. 1 day. Mahaska Co. Death Record.
Shelton, Mrs. Winnie. May 2, 1901. 70 years. Paralysis. Wilson Carey.
Slaughter, Maggie. May 9, 1897.
Smith, Lavada Alice. December 27, 1899. 2 months 21 days. Lung. Wells Co. (Daughter Of James).
Smith, James. September 11, 1887. 20 years. Malaria Fever. McCurdy Funeral Home.
Smith, Mrs. Millie. September 22, 1897. 62 years. Paralysis. Theo. Lofland.
Smith, Morton. Black. March 15, 1884. 22 years. Lung Fever. McCurdy Funeral Home.
Sneede, Helen. December 1, 1887. 1 year 3 months. Measles. McCurdy Funeral Home.
Snody, Sadie. Black. April 2, 1888. 4 years. Burned. McCurdy Funeral Home.
Southall, Ella. March 8, 1901. 12 years. Bowels. W.A. Wells Co.
Southall, Henry. June 12, 1901. 13 years 5 months. Gun Accident. Carey, Wells Co.
Sowyer, Samuel G. January 11, 1883. Son of S. & A. Sowyer.
Spears, Mrs. John (Anna). Black. August 17, 1889. 20 years 4 months 6 days. Malaria Fever. McCurdy Funeral Home.
Spears, John P. Black. October 15, 1889. 30 years. Typhoid Fever. McCurdy Funeral Home.
Spears, Mable. Black. August 23, 1889. 8 days. McCurdy Funeral Home.
Staples, Sallie. Black. May 14, 1900. 22 years. Bowels. W.A.WellsCo.
Tate, Mary Susan. Black. October 4, 1892. 51 years. Accident. McCurdy Funeral Home.
Taylor, Unnamed.* October 30, 1882. 15 months 3 days. Mahaska Co. Death Record.
Thomas, Baby. March 31, 1901. 1 day. Evan Thomas.
Toler, Edward. Black. February 26, 1896. 1 year 10 months. Wm. Toler.
Tolliver, Ben. Black. March 22, 1884. 33 years. Pleurisy. McCurdy Funeral Home.
Tovera, Beulah. August 13, 1898.
Turner, Elnora. May 17, 1901. 30 years 2 months 15 days. St. Vitas' Dance. Callus Green.

LeeAnn Simmers Dickey

Turner, Infant of G. W. Black. October 31, 1889. 16 days. McCurdy Funeral Home.
Turner, Thomas. June 4, 1900. 37 years. Dropsy. Wilson Carey.
Turner, Willis. November 22, 1900. 33 years. Mine Accident. Wilson Carey.
Tyrell, John E. April 6, 1895. 14 years 6 months 10 days. Lung. G.O. Tyrell.
Unknown. Black. July 6, 1884. 1 year. Spinal. McCurdy Funeral Home.
Unknown. December 7, 1890. McCurdy Funeral Home.
Unknown. December 28, 1894. W.A. Wells Co.
Unknown. January 6, 1895. W.A. Wells Co.
Unknown. March 21, 1898. W.A. Wells Co.
Unknown. March 1, 1900. 1 year. W.A. Wells Co.
Unknown. March 28, 1901. W.A. Wells Co.
Unknown. Black. January 1902. McCurdy Funeral Home.
Unknown Baby. May 23, 1897. 5 months. W.A. Wells Co.
Unknown Baby. June 9, 1897. 3 months. W.A. Wells Co.
Unknown Baby. July 21, 1897. W.A. Wells Co.
Unknown Baby. January 19, 1901. W.A. Wells Co.
Unknown Child. January 7, 1887. 5 years.
Unknown Child. June 25, 1898. W.A. Wells Co.
Unknown Infant. February 27, 1901. W.A. Wells Co.
Veney, Albert. Black. September 24, 1886. 32 years. Fever. McCurdy Funeral Home.
Walker, Alfred. April 13, 1900. 6 months. W.A. Wells Co.
Walker, Frankie Rhode. July 16, 1901. 1 year 1 month. Cholera Infantum. Monroe Co. W.E. Gladwin.
Walker, George. Black. May 5, 1896. 60 years 1 month 4 days. Dropsy. Wife.
Walker, George A. Black. February 4, 1887. 35 years. Erysipelas. McCurdy Funeral Home.
Walker, George J. Black. June 13, 1893. 22 years. Mine Accident. McCurdy Funeral Home.
Walker, Mrs. Lydia. Black. June 11, 1896. 31 years 9 months. Consumption. Charles Walker.
Walker, Nellie. February 3, 1900. 21 days. Spasms. W.A. Wells Co.
Watkins, Sam. Black. January 24, 1901. Abt. 52 years. Pneumonia. Monroe Co.-Carey Wilson.
Watkins, Susie. May 26, 1897. 4 years 1 month. Spasms. Sam Watkins.
Wayland, Twin of Laura. Black. July 29, 1885. 7 months. Dysentery. McCurdy Funeral Home.

Before Buxton: The Muchakinock Years

Wells, Unknown. July 27, 1894. W.A. Wells Co.
Wells, Infant. June 9, 1897.
Wells, Infant. July 21, 1897.
Wells, Infant. May 23, 1897.
White, John. Black. May 15, 1894. 35 years. Asthma. W.A. Wells Co.
White, Mrs. Lena. November 9, 1899. 39 years. Typhoid Malaria.
White, Oscar. August 21, 1900. 14 years. Drowned. Dock White.
White, Samuel. Black. October 26, 1884. 3 months. McCurdy Funeral Home.
Wiles, Mrs. L. A. December 14, 1895. F.A. Coleman.
William, Mrs. John. May 16, 1891.
Williams, Daughter of H. A. August 18, 1884. 1½ years. McCurdy Funeral Home.
Williams, Elizabeth. November 13, 1899. 45 years. Dropsy. Sidney Williams.
Williams, F. C. * February 21, 1890. 30 years 1 month 26 days.
Williams, Lizzie. November 12, 1899. 70 years. Mahaska Co. Death Record.
Williams, Mrs. John. * May 16, 1891. No age given.
Williams, T. C. (Frank). February 21, 1890. 30 years 1 month 26 days. Heart. McCurdy Funeral Home. Wife: Millie.
Willis, Betty. Black. January 10, 1884. 7 years 4 months 8 days. Fever. McCurdy Funeral Home.
Willis, Patsey. Black. December 19, 1887. 38 years. Illusion of Brain. McCurdy Funeral Home.
Willis, Randolph. March 14, 1897. 57 years 2 months 12 days. Bronchitis. C.R. Foster.
Wilson, Child of Jacob. Black. July 25, 1886. 2½ years. McCurdy Funeral Home.
Wilson, Harry. March 5, 1914. 1 day. Mahaska Co. Death Record.
Wilson, Josephine. September 27, 1898. 1 year 3 months 17 days. Mahaska Co. Death Record.
Wilson, Mary (Mariah). May 13, 1901. Abt. 41 years. Apoplexy/ Obstetric. Monroe Co.- Jake Wilson.
Winston, Eliza A.* Black. May 9, 1884. 19 years 5 months. Consumption. McCurdy Funeral Home.
Winston, Infant of N.* December 3, 1886. 4 days. Child of I.N. & R.N. Winston.
Winston, Leola A.* February 11, 1885. 1 month 9 days. Debility. Daughter of I.N. & R.N. Winston.
Winston, Mrs. Mary R. June 2, 1888. 21 years 5 days. Consumption. McCurdy Funeral Home.

Wood, Elizabeth T. Black. October 8, 1892. 61 years 11 months. Heart Disease. McCurdy Funeral Home.

Wood, William H. Black. December 20, 1892. 23 years. Stomach. McCurdy Funeral Home.

Woodfolk, Celesta.* Black. October 6, 1882. 43 years. Consumption. McCurdy- Wife of Nelson.

Woodfolk, Ellanora.* 1886.

Woodfolk, Mary.* Black. January 30, 1886. 18 years. Consumption. McCurdy Funeral Home.

Woods, Mrs. Josie. Black. April 6, 1893. 20 years 8 months 10 days. Typhoid Fever. McCurdy Funeral Home.

Woody, William. March 6, 1890.

According to the Oskaloosa newspaper, Fox Chief Cooper (death record listed on page 78) was associated with a medicine show that came to town. The show had planned on being in town for two weeks, giving small performances and peddling Kickapoo Indian Sagwa. Made of barks, roots, and herbs, sagwa was said to be a cure-all for any ailment. After he was in town for one week, someone gave Chief Cooper a flask of Muchakinock's double distilled whiskey, known as Senegambian Fire Water.

His body was found the next morning and he was buried in the Muchakinock Cemetery. Reportedly he was placed in a standing position, though no one seems to know why.

Before Buxton: The Muchakinock Years

Sources

Cooks vs. Cutts -- Papers and testimony in the contest election case of J. C. Cook vs. M. E. Cutts, from the Sixth Congressional District of Iowa. January 16, 1882- Serial Set Vol. No 2042

Eddyville *Tribune* newspaper

Oskaloosa *Herald* 1876- 1920

From Indian Village to Muchakinock to Buxton -- Mahaska County Historical Society, Fall 2008

Sanborn Fire Maps 1895 and 1900

Iowa State *Bystander* newspaper

Mahaska County Marriage Records 1870- 1930

Mahaska, Monroe, Wapello County Death Records 1870- 1930

History of Coal Mining in Iowa by James H. Lees

LeeAnn Simmers Dickey

About the Author

Lee Ann Simmers Dickey is a dedicated genealogist who started researching her own family tree and ended up seeking out records and documentation for families across the nation. She is also a proud mother and grandmother.

She is also the author of BUXTON ROOTS, which includes marriage, death, and census records from Buxton, Iowa; BUXTON BRANCHES, which includes birth records from Buxton, Iowa; and EDDYVILLE, a history of the small town which is partly in Mahaska County, partly in Monroe County, and partly in Wapello County Iowa.

For more information about these and other books, calendars and products, visit
www.pbllimited.com
PBL Limited
P.O. Box 935
Ottumwa Iowa 52501

www.ingramcontent.com/pod-product-compliance
Lightning Source LLC
Chambersburg PA
CBHW080252170426
43192CB00014BA/2657